THE STYLE GUIDE

is a book for fashion conscious teenagers. It tells you about colour. What colours can you wear and what colours should you steer clear of? It tells you about shapes. Should you wear tight or loose fitting clothes? Should your skirts be long or short? It teaches you how to look after your clothes, and how to dress for that special occasion. There's a fun fashion quiz which tells you how stylish you are, and there's some practical advice in the questions and answers chapter. There's all this plus much more.

Do you ooze style? Read on and find out. If you don't, one thing's for sure — by the time you've finished this book you will!

To Alan, for being Alan

THE *Style* GUIDE

kim martin

Illustrated by Michelle Vincent

Hodder and Stoughton

Text copyright © 1989 by Kim Martin

Illustrations copyright © 1989 Hodder and Stoughton Ltd.

First published in Great Britain in 1989 by Lightning

British Library C.I.P.

Martin, Kim
   The style guide
   1. Fashion
   I. Title
   746.9'2

ISBN 0-340-51104-4

This book is sold subject to the condition that it shall not, by way of trade or otherwise, be lent, re-sold, hired out or otherwise circulated without the publisher's prior consent in any form of binding or cover other than that in which it is published and without a similar condition including this condition being imposed on the subsequent purchaser.

No part of this publication may be reproduced or transmitted in any form or by any means, electronically or mechanically, including photocopying, recording or any information storage or retrieval system, without either the prior permission in writing from the publisher or a licence, permitting restricted copying. In the United Kingdom such licences are issued by the Copyright Licensing Agency, 33–34 Alfred Place, London WC1E 7SP.

Printed and bound in Great Britain for Hodder and Stoughton Children's Books, a division of Hodder and Stoughton Ltd, Mill Road, Dunton Green, Sevenoaks, Kent TN13 2YA. (Editorial Office: 47 Bedford Square, London WC1B 3DP) by Cox and Wyman Ltd, Reading, Berks. Photoset by Rowland Phototypesetting Ltd, Bury St Edmunds, Suffolk.

Contents

What is Style?		7
Chapter One	DRESSING TO SUIT YOUR SHAPE	9
Chapter Two	TALKING SHOP	19
Chapter Three	COLOUR	23
Chapter Four	FIRST IMPRESSIONS	35
Chapter Five	ACCESSORIES	41
Chapter Six	MAKE-UP	53
Chapter Seven	YOUR HOLIDAY WARDROBE	65
Chapter Eight	GLASSES	81
Chapter Nine	STYLE FILE	89
Chapter Ten	SPECIAL OCCASION DRESSING	93
Chapter Eleven	THE STYLE GUIDE QUIZ	99
Chapter Twelve	DOS AND DON'TS	103
Chapter Thirteen	CLOTHES CARE	109
Chapter Fourteen	QUESTIONS AND ANSWERS	115

What is style?

Well I'll start by telling you what it isn't. Style is not wearing something just because it's in fashion. Wearing the latest in designer fashion doesn't have to mean you have style, because it's not *what* you wear but the *way* that you wear it. Style is about wearing clothes that go with your personality, colouring and shape. People with wardrobes full of clothes often declare that they have nothing to wear. So this book will teach you how to mix and match garments in your wardrobe to suit your individual look. Style is about feeling comfortable and good in what you're wearing. If you feel confident in what you're wearing you will carry it off all the better.

So how do you get that confidence? Well it helps if you feel good in yourself. This means not just dressing well, but looking after your body too. Healthy eating and exercise will improve your overall appearance, because good skin and healthy hair depend a lot on your diet. Once you feel a better person, when you take a look at yourself, instead of pulling yourself to pieces you can look at your best features and learn how to make the most of them. When you see what potential you have, with the help of this book you can develop an individual style of your very own.

Chapter One

Dressing to Suit your Shape

Shape Up

Stand naked in front of a full length mirror and take a good look at yourself. Do you really know your body shape and size? Are you honest with yourself? Or when you look at your reflection do you kid yourself that your figure is better than it really is? If the answer is yes, you do kid yourself, don't panic! You'll be interested to find that so do most other people.

Facing up to your shape is the first step to looking good. You need to learn what your good and bad points are, and get to know what does and doesn't suit you. Then you can make the most of your good points and camouflage your bad ones. If you decide that you need to diet, it is best to set yourself a time limit. This way you are more likely to stick to it. It is important however, that you know your build, because if you are big boned or wide hipped for example, no dieting will change this. Therefore you have to accept yourself as you are. Don't let this depress you though, because with a bit of disguise and clever dressing you can look amazing. If you are exceptionally big, tall or small however, you can go to specialist shops which cater just for you. If you are 5ft 3 inches in height or under, you are considered small. 5ft 4 inches to 5ft 7 inches is average and 5ft 8 inches and over is tall.

There are three basic physiological shapes. These are:
ectomorph, which is small framed and slim
mesomorph, which is a medium build and fairly well proportioned and
endomorph, which is a heavy build, plump and curvy.
Some people can be a mixture of shapes.

Don't get blasé about your figure. It is so easy to put on weight without realising. So don't wait until you try on your best suit and find that you can't do the zip up! Keep an eye on your figure and weigh yourself if you feel you have put on a bit of weight. Keep yourself in shape but don't despair if your figure isn't perfect – few people have a perfect figure. Models are an exception, but most of them have to work terribly hard to keep in shape. Looking good is how they make their living, so don't waste time wishing for something you can't have. Make the most of what you've got instead.

Big Build

The cut and detail on an outfit can make a lot of difference to how you look. You should avoid clothes with lots of small details like pockets and trimmings and wear clothes with a generous cut instead. Also avoid any fabrics that cling to the body accentuating any bulk. Wear large bold prints which you can carry off easily.

Small Build

If you are on the small side you should wear neat well cut clothes. Anything on the big side will just swallow you up.

Delicate Features

If you have delicate features, go for delicate fabrics with pretty details.

Big or Small Head

If your head looks too big compared to the rest of your body, keep your hairstyle short, unfussy and neat. If your head looks too small, go for a perm or a hairstyle with lots of volume making your head seem larger.

Long or Short Neck

Long necks can look very graceful, but if yours makes you unhappy, avoid anything that will emphasise the neck's narrowness, such as a polo neck jumper. Never wear a shirt buttoned to the top, go for open-neck shirts instead. If your neck is short, wear tops that keep the neck as bare as possible. Try scooped, square or V-shaped necklines which give an illusion of length. Avoid roll collars or slit necklines which will just draw attention to the neck. Never wear chunky necklaces or scarves. Wear bold earrings instead, drawing the attention to your ears.

Narrow or Wide Shoulders

If you have narrow shoulders you can build them up by wearing a top with shoulder pads. You can buy shoulder pads very cheaply from most haberdashery departments. They come in all different shapes and sizes and some of them have Velcro enabling you to wear them with lots of different tops. Padded shoulders are great for making your waist and hips look slimmer. This is because by contouring the shoulders with shoulder pads they are accentuated, appearing wider than the hips. However, if you have narrow shoulders, it will also mean that you have a narrower neck. So to avoid making your neck look narrower still, you must be careful to get the right balance,

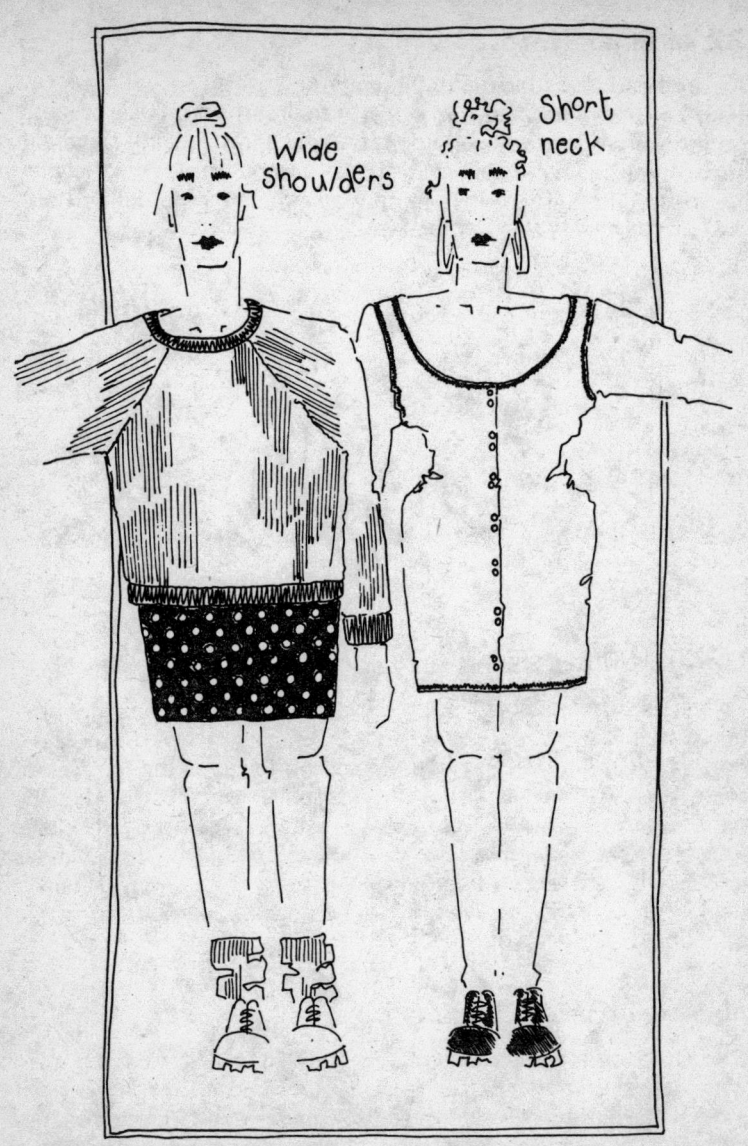

making sure that your shoulder pads aren't too big. Wide shoulders can look good and don't need shoulder pads. However, if you are wide shouldered, there are certain garments that you shouldn't wear. Avoid off the shoulder tops or halter necks and opt for jumpers with raglan sleeves. They play down wide shoulders making them look rounded and narrower than they are.

Big or Small Bust

If your bust is big it is important that you wear a bra that gives you good support and shape. It is also important that it fits properly because squashing yourself into a bra that is too small for you can look very unsightly. If you wear shirts or blouses make sure that they are loose fitting. There is nothing worse than gaping button holes

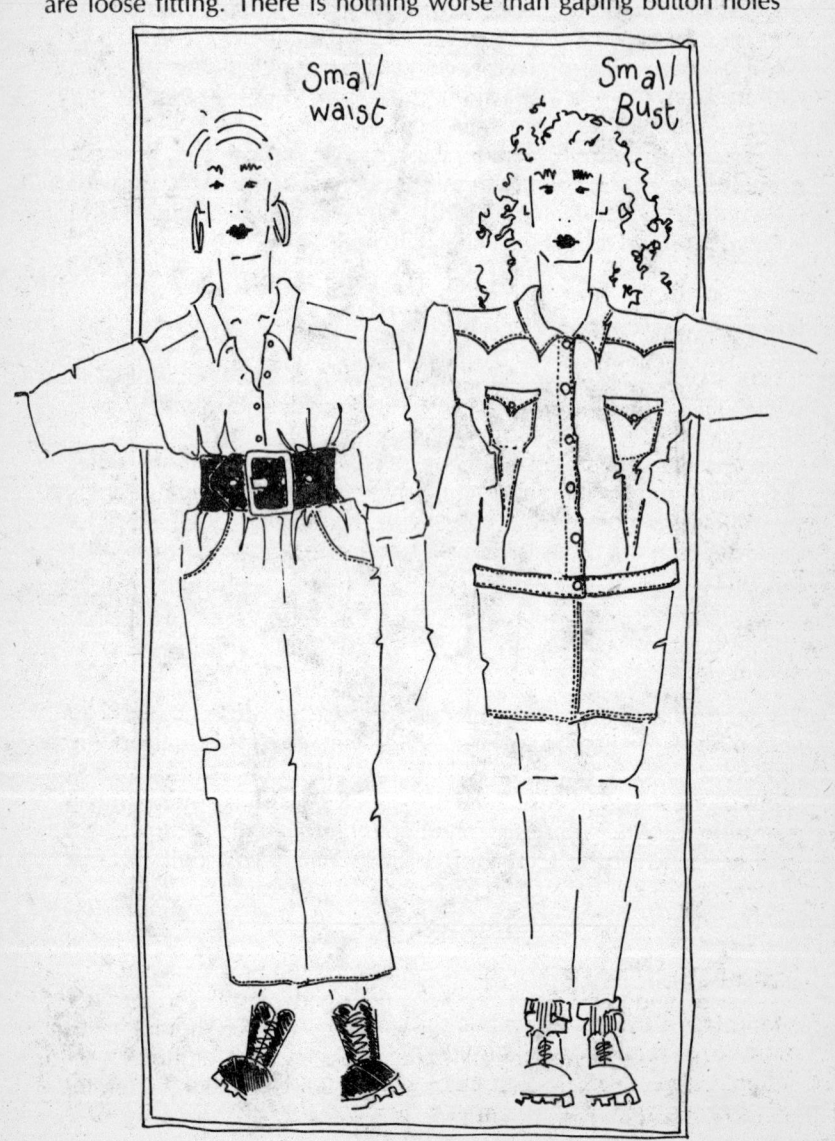

which can look really tarty. Some fitted tops, as long as they are not too fitted, can look really good but you must wear something fitted with confidence to carry it off properly. Don't hunch yourself up, giving yourself round shoulders which many people with big busts seem to do. Walk tall and be proud of your bust. Some fitted tops can show ugly seams on bras so go for a seamless bra for a smoother look. Also avoid clingy tops, especially with vertical stripes. Don't wear anything around your neck because necklaces can draw attention to the bust. Never be tempted to wear garments that can only be worn without a bra. If you wear a slit neck top, pin your bra straps to the inside of the top to prevent them from showing.

If your bust is small, avoid wearing anything low cut. Low cut garments only look good with a bit of a cleavage. Go for shirts or jackets with pockets over the bustline instead and wear a padded bra – it will make your bust look slightly bigger.

Big or Small Waist

If you have a small waist make the most of it and show it off with a wide belt. Go for fitted skirts and trousers, especially jodhpurs which can look amazing.

If you have a big waist avoid waisted clothes and opt for clothes that fall from the shoulders to a narrow hemline. Or wear jumpers that fall below the waistline. Never wear belts around your waist but wear them on the hips instead, detracting the eyes away from your big area.

A Big Bottom Half

Wide hips, thighs and a big bottom are the most common of complaints. You can make the area look smaller by making your top half look bigger. Wear shoulder pads and light colours on top drawing the eye upwards. Steer clear of clingy fabrics and wear well cut straight skirts with square shouldered tops. Avoid drop waisted garments and pockets on the hips which will just pull the eye downwards. Go for long square shaped jackets instead.

Fat or Thin Legs

If your legs are fat never wear a short skirt or dainty shoes. You will only make your legs look fatter. Dark tights will make your legs look slimmer, and dark tights and shoes in the same shade will make your legs look longer. If your legs are too thin wear fairly long skirts. Never wear full skirts because they make your legs look even thinner. If you want to wear a short skirt do so, but wear textured tights or ones with horizontal stripes. This will make your legs appear more shapely. (See illustration on page 11).

Chapter Two

Talking Shop

Best Buys

There are so many shops to choose from and so many different styles in the shops, so where do you start? First of all you should think about what you really need. Are you buying clothes for everyday wear or are you buying something for a special occasion? If you are buying for a special occasion be practical. Will you wear the outfit again or will it sit in your wardrobe and then be out of date the next time you go to wear it? If you choose carefully you can get something that can be dressed up or down enabling you to wear the outfit for evening and daywear.

Before you go shopping make a list of what you really need. Go through your wardrobe and make a note of the colours that dominate your wardrobe. By choosing sensibly you will probably find that you can mix and match your outfit around with several garments in your wardrobe creating lots of different looks. If you are buying clothes for everyday wear think about where you'll be wearing it. If you work, how presentable do you have to be? If you choose a pale colour will it get grubby really quickly?

If you go into a shop and there is so much to choose from that you become overwhelmed by it all and uncertain about what to buy, don't buy anything because mistakes can be costly. The best thing to do is go away and give yourself time to think and maybe go back to the shop half an hour later, but only if you really want something. You don't have to buy something just because it's there.

Don't let shop assistants intimidate you either. This is very easily done after dashing around the shops and maybe getting caught in the rain. You feel like a wreck while the shop assistant looks immaculate and relaxed. To make things worse there are posters of size 8 models looking sophisticated and staring you right in the face. Don't let this get you down. Just tell yourself that in the real world people are size 12 upwards.

If you see something that you love instantly then buy it. Don't make the mistake of thinking about it because when you go back it might not be there. Anything that you want instantly is usually a good buy.

If you are bad with money set yourself a price limit before you go out and stick to it. It is so easy to get carried away when buying more than one item. If you're spending a lot of money on a garment be sure to check the quality of it. Something that looks nice at a glance can turn out to be badly made when looked at more closely.

Wear It Well

Never buy anything without trying it on first. When you try it on don't just stand in front of the mirror. Move around in the outfit to see if it feels comfortable, because if it feels uncomfortable you probably won't wear it. Note how the outfit hangs and if it is the right length. If it needs shortening make sure there isn't any detail that would be lost, like pleats, stitching or pockets. If you're buying a skirt sit down in it to see how comfortable it feels. Skirts also ride up when sitting so make sure it isn't too short. If you've got a new pair of shoes to wear with your outfit then take them shopping with you so you can try them on with the outfit to see the complete look.

In The Wash

When buying a garment check the label for washing instructions. Some items say 'Dry Clean Only' which is OK for certain garments but not very practical if the item happens to be say a white shirt. It would obviously need cleaning after each wear and would prove very expensive. Check jumper labels to see if they can be machine washed and tumble dried otherwise you could end up with a jumper to fit your old Sindy doll!

Sales

Shops have sales at the end of a season because they need to make room for the new season's fashions. Buyers can sometimes over anticipate how a garment is going to sell and order too many. Or it could be that people simply haven't got much money to spend because of inflation and therefore the shop's stock isn't selling. Because of this we can buy things at reduced prices.

Some sale items are not particularly desirable and that is why nobody has bought them. However, if you shop carefully there are bargains to be found. The best buys are basics like shirts and jumpers and classics like blazers that can be worn and worn. Steer clear of very trendy items and 'this season's' colour. If it's the end of the season the clothes will be on their way out and most certainly be old hat by next season.

Don't buy something just because it's in the sale. You probably won't wear it that much and then it isn't such a bargain after all. In fact some much more expensive clothes will turn out to be more economical even if they're not in the sale. If you choose carefully you can buy something very classic which will last you for years.

Chapter Three

The Meaning of Colour

The Meaning of Colour

What is colour? Colour is a sensation produced in the eye by rays of decomposed light. Well, that's what the dictionary says! Colour is all around us. Just think how dull the world would be if we didn't have it. There'd be no bright blue skies, sunsets or pretty gardens. Colour plays a bigger part in our lives than most people realise and it is very important in fashion. Simply by changing its colour you can transform a dreary outfit into an amazing one. Colours can even determine your mood. Some colours can make you feel very happy while others make you feel very sad. Whether colour excites or depresses you, one thing is certain – it's too important to be ignored.

Popular Colours

Red is one of the most popular colours. It stands for vitality and happiness. It's a hot colour highly charged with emotion. Red also speaks of danger and many warning signs are made in red. When you think of red you think of glowing fires and sunsets. Did you know that being surrounded by red actually makes your heart beat faster and your temperature rise releasing boosts of adrenalin into the bloodstream? It is a colour that can look amazing on the right person – usually a soft red looks best. You have to be daring to wear red because it's a colour that gets you noticed!

Purple is the colour that was worn by Kings. It's the colour of luxury. Purple looks great for evening wear in rich velvets. Wearing purple shows that you are a leader and very daring.

Blue is a very popular colour to wear because there are so many shades to choose from. The colour ranges from pastel blue to electric blue so there's a tone to suit all colourings. Blue can make us feel many things. It can lift up our spirits when we wake up and see a clear blue sky or it can make us feel sad. Blue is also very calming to the eye and can ease high blood pressure. But too much blue can be cold and uninviting.

Green is a clean fresh colour. It is the colour of Spring, relaxing and peaceful. Although it isn't a primary colour it looks good with red, blue and yellow. Different shades of green can look good together, or try green with aqua blue. It's a very subtle colour with a shade to flatter any type of colouring but it looks especially good on red heads. Green can also look great for evening wear in silks and velvet.

Yellow is the colour of sunshine and happiness. It makes us think of summer and golden beaches. The deeper the yellow the brighter it appears, reflecting so much light that it cannot be ignored. Yellow can only be worn by very few people so if you're pale skinned steer clear of it. However, if you tan easily go for yellow because no other colour looks nicer with a tan. Be certain though, that it's the right shade. When yellow reflects the light it makes your skin tone look bleached out and grey if you're not careful. It is probably safer to wear just one item of yellow rather than a whole outfit.

White is for weddings. For long floating satin dresses and pearls. White makes you think of everything fresh and clean. Nothing looks smarter than a crisp cotton shirt in white. White makes you think of sophistication, elegance and femininity. Nothing is prettier and more feminine than white lace. But white has to be worn with care otherwise it won't stay white for very long! It should also only be worn if you are slim (unless it's very loose fitting) because it can show every spare ounce of flesh on your body and not be very flattering at all. If you think you've got what it takes to wear white team it with primary colours or go for the nautical look with navy and white stripes.

Pink they say, makes boys wink! Pastel pink is feminine and pretty, while fuchsia is vibrant and exciting and bound to get you noticed. It's the colour that spells fun but not many people can really carry it off. Fuchsia looks better worn at a minimum rather than a head to toe outfit. Try teaming fuchsia accessories with black or white for a simple but stunning effect.

Black is worn by almost everybody. It is popular because you don't have to spend ages choosing items to match it. Almost anything can look good with black, in fact it's one of the easiest colours to wear. The black leather jacket has been with us for years and what about the faithful black dress? Almost every girl has at least one black dress in her wardrobe. It can be dressed up or down depending on the occasion. You can look sexy in black or powerful in a smart suit. Whatever the fabric, black makes you look classy.

Colours and Your Personality

Did you know that the colours that you wear can reveal your true personality? Well, read on and find out some very interesting things about yourself!

Primary Colours

If you love primary colours you are a very happy sociable person. People like being with you because of your enthusiasm and bright ideas. You're the one in charge, the ring leader. You're the one that people look to when planning to go somewhere for some entertainment. You've always got something interesting up your sleeve. When you go out for the evening one of the best parts of it for you is the dressing up. You love gossiping, playing the fool and telling jokes. People enjoy being entertained by you because you are such an extrovert. You're always making new friends because people find you very easy to talk to. You're a person that makes quick snap decisions because you're quite impatient by nature, and when occasionally you get things wrong you find it difficult admitting your mistakes. Your life style is very action packed. You're a real outdoors kind of person and love competing in most sports. You're a bit of a risk taker. You attract people wherever you go with your confident and bubbly personality.

You are terribly ambitious and would love to be extremely rich and famous. You will be successful in most things because you're a good talker and a 'go getter'. However, you must be careful of becoming too overpowering. If you're a little too ambitious people might be a bit overwhelmed by you. You're also a very impulsive person. If you fall for somebody you aren't afraid to make the first move. Being very generous you love showering people with gifts.

If you're into primaries you'll look good in

>bold patterns
>checks
>tartans
>stripes.

Wear bright party dresses with fun accessories. You also have the confidence to carry off wearing a hat so wear one to finish the look with style.

Earthy Colours

If you go for earthy colours, you're a person of good taste. You go for quality rather than quantity. You'd much rather buy one expensive jumper than four cheap ones. You only like the good things in life. With jewellery, you go for the real thing and not imitations. And the same goes for food. You only eat fresh healthy food which is very wholesome, there's no hamburgers for you.

You're what people think of as a real friend. People know that you are loyal and that they can trust you. They know that they can tell you their innermost secrets without having to worry that you'll spread gossip as soon as their backs are turned. You're an honest person because deceiving just isn't in your nature. If friends make mistakes you're very tactful and can give good sound advice. You're also a good shoulder to cry on. You love socialising and your idea of a good evening out is anywhere where there is good conversation. You're not into discos. You're a very intelligent person and you don't make decisions quickly. You hate making mistakes so when making a decision you always take your time weighing up the pros and cons. If you do make a mistake you're the first to admit it. Being quietly ambitious, you're not an exhibitionist and hate any fuss. You'll succeed although you're probably not bold or loud enough to go to the very top.

You're a bit of a romantic and are a very caring person although you can be cautious in love. Your partner will probably be your best friend because you're a very communicative person. You take love very seriously indeed although you're an extremely calm and laid back person. Maybe too laid back. It might be an idea to start exercising because you spend so much time being concerned about other people that you neglect your own health.

If you're into earthy colours you'll look good in

> rust
> coffee
> dark chocolate
> classic shapes

Go for good quality leggings and chunky sweaters for a really cosy look.

Clashy Colours

Do you wear colours that clash? If you do then you are the kind of person that will try anything once. You are a person that is very daring. You are a real individual and a bit of a split personality too. One minute you're being a real loudmouth and the next you're quiet and by yourself. You're a colourful character that people love to watch. Some people might say that you're a little crazy. You're the kind of person that loves to do things on the spur of the moment. One minute you'll be indoors watching television and the next you could decide to go to the seaside for the day. You love adventure and will always be at 'the' social event – even if you're not invited you'll find a way of bluffing your way in! Your life is just one big surprise and you can never stick to any one thing for too long. You have many different circles of friends to fit your different moods and you change your job like the weather. You also love to travel to see as many places as you can.

You'll do anything to be different and that includes clothes. You wear what you want when you want even if it's totally inappropriate. You love being dramatic and are always out to shock. You can be very deep one minute and come up with crazy ideas the next.

You're a very creative person and would be good in any artistic job. You could even be an inventor. Money isn't important to you at all. You are much more interested in variety and excitement. You're the kind of person that would pack up work and travel the world if you became bored with your job. You would also be much more suited to working on your own rather than in a team. This is because of your ever changing personality.

To have a successful relationship with somebody would mean finding a person as unpredictable as yourself. You are so over the top that anybody with a shy nature would be completely embarrassed by you. You're probably too unsettled to get to know anybody seriously but when you do fall in love it will be love at first sight. If you're into clashy colours you'll look good in

> bold stripes
> clashing spots
> loud patterns.

Wear fuchsia, orange, turquoise and lime for a dazzling look that will always make you stand out in the crowd.

Pastel Colours

If soft pastels are for you, you are a person of kind nature. You love animals and they equally love you. You are very good with children and they love having your attention. With your great patience you can spend hours telling fairytales and playing games.

You are a very good listener and friends are always pouring out their troubles to you. This is because they know they can trust you. You are quite a sensitive vulnerable person and are easily hurt and upset, so sometimes you could do with a shoulder to cry on yourself. You're the kind of person that people like to protect because you are a very shy person, warm and unthreatening. You're a real romantic and live in a kind of fairytale world. You read love stories, listen to romantic songs and watch old romantic movies on television.

When you fall in love you fall hook line and sinker, and your partner can do no wrong in your eyes. You are kind, almost too kind, and some people may take advantage of you. You are always ready to forgive when maybe forgiveness isn't due. You're not particularly ambitious and really just want a stable and secure life. So you love to be surrounded by your family and friends. You have a bit of an artistic streak. You are quite good with your hands and enjoy making things.

If you're into pastels you'll look good in

>   florals
>   floaty fabrics
>   frills
>   lace
>   broderie anglaise.

Soft pastels such as powder blue, lemon, peach and apricot look great on you worn in layers. Go for soft fabrics such as suede, lambswool, satin and silk. For evenings choose velvet for a stunning effect.

Colours and Patterns

Patterns can liven up a dull wardrobe. Today we are much more adventurous and we mix many different patterns. With computer-aided design and colour printing there are a lot more patterns to choose from. The variety on offer is endless and exciting. The more colours there are in a pattern the easier it is to find accessories to match.

Pile on layers of winter woollies with a colour or pattern link. If you wear say a red, blue and white patterned jumper, wear red and blue leggings and accessories to match, keeping the pattern similar. If you're in the mood for fun go for spots. There's polka dots or big spots to choose from but if that doesn't tickle your fancy try some stripes. There's vertical, horizontal, wide stripes or pinstripes, something to suit everyone. Add a stripy top to a plain outfit, it can work wonders. Try adding a red and white top to faded denim for a clean and casual look.

If your jacket has an interesting lining turn back your cuffs so the lining is revealed. Match your outfit to one of the colours in the lining and you'll look great. Try making an old suit look more interesting by wearing it with a patterned shirt. Wear accessories to pick up the colours in the pattern and you'll have a new look. Patterns like colours can also reveal your true personality. Extroverts wear stripes and loud checks while quieter types opt for flowers, animal shapes, pinstripes, paisleys and tweeds.

Pattern Tips

* Mixed patterns look best when there is one main colour linking all the garments together.

* If you're wearing something with a large print, keep your jewellery and accessories to a minimum because nothing looks worse than a cluttered look.

* Small patterns can look elegant and have a slimming effect while large patterns look stunning but can make you look big.

* Wavy lines can add curves to a slim figure.

* Spots and stripes look good mixed together for a fun and sporty look.

* Mix large checks with small checks in the same colourway for an individual look.

* Be daring and wear the same pattern in two different colourways.

* Wear tartan with houndstooth checks, it looks better than you'd think.

* Wear large prints but keep the design of your outfit simple and unfussy.

* If you think you look too tall and skinny wear a big spotted loose top with a bright coloured background.

* To look taller and slimmer wear light coloured polka dots on a dark background.

* Wear vertical stripes to look thinner and horizontal stripes to look bigger. Horizontal stripes do wonders for a small bust while diagonal stripes in leggings or tights can make skinny legs look very shapely.

Colours To Suit You

Take a good look at yourself in a mirror. Do you look as good as you possibly could? If you don't like what you see in your reflection, if you feel ugly and hate your complexion, it could be solved very simply. You're probably just wearing the wrong colours to go with your skin tone, hair and eyes. You see, the colour that you wear is more important than you think. So you can't just throw on a jumper because you like its colour because the colour might not like you. You have to discover what colours flatter you if you want to be sure to look your best. So how do you decide what colours suit you? Read on and find out.

The first step is to find out what colour your skin tone actually is. It isn't just a matter of having white, black or olive skin. It's a lot more complex than that. Your complexion is either yellow or blue based and it is these undertones in our skin which affect how we look in certain colours. If your complexion is yellow based your skin has warm undertones and if it is blue based it has cool undertones.

So how do you find out what your skin type is? Well if just looking in a mirror doesn't give you an answer it could be that you're a borderline case having cool and warm undertones. This means that you suit most cool and warm colours. If you're a little confused by what cool and warm colours actually are here's a list to help you. Warm colours include navy, shades of grey, blue, as well as grass greens, peach, coral, turquoise, beige, and tan. Cool colours are, cornflower blue, emerald green, pastel pinks, silver grey and brights like acid lemon. If however you aren't a borderline case and find it difficult deciding what skin type you are, try applying two different tones of foundation to your face, putting a warm pink on one cheek and a cool beige on the other. Now you will be able to see which skin type you are. Now that you know your skin type you can double check this method by holding yellow and blue based items against your skin. The correct base tones will harmonise with your skin making your skin have a healthy glow, whilst the wrong colour will make your complexion look pale, sallow and can even age you. If you have discovered your skin tones but are still a little confused as to what colours suit you, follow these simple guidelines:

* **Brunettes, ashbrowns and blondes** with fair or pink complexions and eyes of blue, blue-grey, aqua or hazel look best in cool pastel colours and soft neutrals. These colours will make your skin look smooth, clear and blemish free. Go for white, pearly pink, pastel pink, shocking pink, mushroom, grey, blue-greys, denim blue, browns, green-blue, navy, airforce blue, sky blue, powder blue, lavender, burgundy, aqua, purple, red browns, sea green, mint or jade.

* **If you have light brown, raven or grey hair** with an olive to dark complexion and your eyes are dark blue, grey-green, grey-brown or grey-blue you'll look good in bright vivid or icy colours with a sharp contrast. Choose charcoal, taupe, silver grey, black, navy,

electric-blue, royal blue, ice blue, ice violet, fuchsia, acid lemon, bright orange, red, white, sea green, emerald, purple and claret.

* **Is your hair red, auburn, golden brown or chestnut brown?** Do you have freckles with a peaches and cream or pale complexion? Are your eyes green or brown? If you fit any of these descriptions you'll look best in rich warm earthy and vibrant colours. Try tan, camel, oatmeal, beige, gold, bronze, chestnut, coffee, chocolate, salmon, apricot, ginger, peach, cinnamon orange, coral, rust, tomato red, terracotta, mustard, lime, olive, cream, turquoise and periwinkle blue.

* **Golden blondes, strawberry blondes, mid browns and carrot redheads** with peachy beige, or creamy ivory complexions, and eyes of clear blue, green, aqua, hazel or golden brown look prettiest in warm colours. These are tomato red, bright coral, cinnamon, gold, mustard, turquoise, beige, black, violet, periwinkle blue, terracotta, peach, tangerine, salmon and apricot.

Colours That Go Together

The key to looking good isn't just wearing the colours that suit you. Wearing colours that go together is equally important. You wouldn't for example wear bright orange with pastel pink. Well, I hope you wouldn't! If you go for vivid colours the shade should be of equal intensity. Your outfit will look silly if you team bright blue with bright green and a not so bright yellow. The same goes for pastels. Wear layers of baby blue, pastel pink and lemon, making sure the tones are equally matched for a lovely fresh look. Or go for a classy look in warm earthy colours. Khaki, cream and chocolate brown are a winning combination.

Cream: A nice earthy colour which looks great with beige, green, black and burnt orange. Avoid wearing white with cream because it will just make the cream look dirty and off colour.

Grey: Looks good mixed with quite a few different colours. One of my favourite combinations is grey and red. In fact any shade of red looks good with grey. Or try adding white, violet, black or purple, as they all blend perfectly.

Navy: Nothing in my opinion goes better with navy than white. The nautical look re-emerges each summer and never fails to look smart and fun. Other colours that look good with navy are shades of pink, red, yellow or sky blue.

Burgundy: A winter colour which looks great with any shade of grey, cream or pink. It also looks rather interesting with bottle green.

White: The most popular summer colour. It looks good with pastels like dusty pinks and powder blue. It also looks equally as good with brights.

Stone: This can look good worn with navy. Stone trousers worn with a navy blazer are a perfect blend. Accessorise with red and white for a stylish look.

Finally, if you're trying out a new colour, don't spend a fortune on an outfit until you're sure the colour works. Start with a small item like a jumper or shirt until you're really sure that the colour is for you. Secondly, don't get carried away mixing too many colours together. They might blend nicely but you can have too much of a good thing. Most people look their best when wearing no more than three colours. You'll usually find that a limited number of colours work best although there are occasional exceptions. Lastly, try to avoid wearing a complete outfit in just one colour because it will look too contrived.

Slimming Colours

The eye is attracted to bright colours so if you are big you should avoid wearing them. Pale colours give an illusion of space, also making you look big. Darker colours, however, make you look slimmer because they make an area appear smaller than it is. So if you want to look slimmer, go for dark toned colours rather than lighter ones. A good trick is to wear darker tones on trouble areas using brighter colours elsewhere. This attracts the eye away from your trouble areas.

What To Wear From Season To Season

Summer

Summer is here so grab your shorts and a T-shirt in bright yellow to match the sun. As I said before, nothing looks better than yellow with a tan. Or go for crisp white, teamed with blue or denim for a completely fresh look.

Winter

Winter is with us which can mean snow. Go for mittens and woollies in loud ski colours for a fun look. Winter also means Christmas and the season for parties. So, leave the baggy jumpers behind and step into a clingy party dress in red, mauve or blue depending on your skin tone.

Spring

Go mad with pastels because spring is in the air. Pile everything on in layers using all the baby soft colours available. Wear pastel woolly tights because the sun has returned but there's still a bit of a chill. Or go for faded denim with a pretty pink floral shirt to match the flowers in bloom.

Autumn

It's autumn and the leaves are falling. Go for warm earthy colours. Wear little skirts with leggings and cosy jumpers in oranges and browns to match the leaves on the ground.

Rules Are Meant To Be Broken

Any colour rule can be broken as long as you know what you're doing. It's all to do with timing, if the colour is right for the moment. A lot depends on the strength of the colours as to whether they'll work together. Be daring and brave and go for a new exciting look. Once you've changed your look and gone mad with your clothes and colour, go mad with your hair too. Make it wild to go with your outfit. Add some bold jewellery and bright make-up and you'll see that fashion can be fun!

Chapter Four

First Impressions

The way we dress says a lot about our personality. We cannot change our body shape in a drastic way. If we have big hips for example, we have to live with them. We can however give an impression simply by the way we dress. When we first meet a person we have an impression of them after about three minutes, simply by taking into account what they are wearing and how they are wearing it. To prove this theory, I am going to put it into practice.

Clothes Talk

Imagine that you are going on a blind date. You are meeting a boy outside your local cinema and it has been arranged by your best friend. You have never met this boy before. While you are waiting, you spot a boy in a tailored suit looking very well groomed. You instantly think that he is respectable, reliable, honest, sensible and quite sophisticated. You then spot a boy that is wearing faded jeans, a leather biker jacket and chunky shoes. 'This boy looks like he could be a laugh', you think to yourself. He doesn't look the boring stuck in a rut sort. He looks like he takes a keen interest in fashion and probably music. He lives life to the full, leading an active social life, going to gigs and the cinema on a regular basis. Lastly, you spot a boy in cords, a second-hand tweed coat and battered trainers. 'This boy looks like a student', you think. Studying is his main priority. He gets a grant, but has more important things to spend his money on than clothes. He's so wrapped up in his books that he wouldn't know what was fashionable if it stared him right in the face. Clothes are just hassle as far as he is concerned. So you see, just by dressing in a certain style, it can say a lot about your personality.

Just The Job

If you were going for a job interview, and the job that you were applying for was a very high powered one, what would you wear to the interview?
A) A smart tailored suit with a formal shirt underneath, tights and small heels.
B) A frilly blouse teamed with a pretty floral print skirt, no tights and sandals.

You might think that both outfits are OK. After all, a blouse and a floral skirt are hardly scruffy. However, if you were to choose B) you would give the impression of being friendly, gentle and caring with a passive nature. You wouldn't look terribly efficient, and the company wouldn't have much confidence. If however you were to wear A) you'd look sharp, strong, decisive and in control. You would be far more likely to get the job.

Take One Black Dress

It isn't just the clothes you wear that give an impression. Hair, make-up and accessories play an important part too. Here we take one black dress, and style it to give it three completely different looks:

1. Team the black dress with a cropped fitted jacket, black suede sling back shoes, black sheer tights, large hoop earrings and lots of bracelets. Wear brightly coloured lipstick and style your hair in a flamboyant way.

2. Team the black dress with a faded denim jacket, chunky shoes and woolly tights. Wear a soft coloured lipstick and style your hair in a high ponytail.

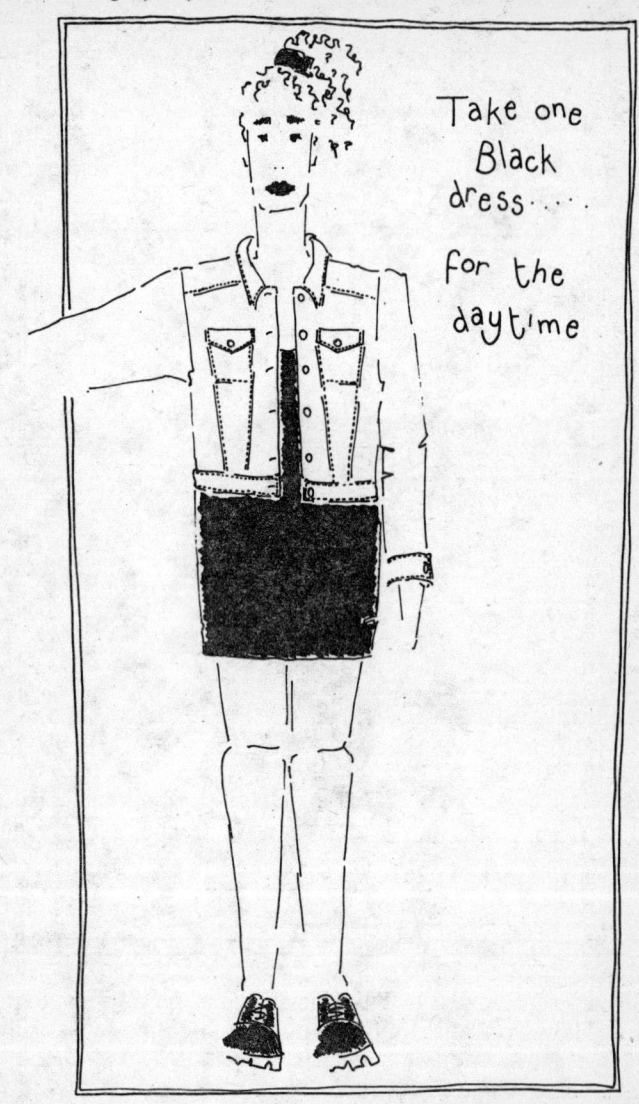

Take one Black dress.... for the daytime

3. Team the black dress with a smart tailored jacket, loafers, opaque tights and clip on earrings. Wear a natural coloured lipstick and style your hair off your face, wearing it in a large hair clip at the back.

Take one Black dress......

for the office

So now you can see that with the clever use of accessories, hair and make-up, how you can create three totally different looks with the same black dress.

The first look is an evening look. It gives the impression that you're an extrovert, looking for a night of excitement.

The second look is a casual daytime or weekend look. It's casual but stylish and gives the impression that you're a girl that's going places.

The third look is a smart office look. This look gives the impression that you are professional and steadfast.

Style Without Cash

You don't have to be trendy to make a good impression. You don't need lots of money either. You can look stylish by simply setting your own style and choosing a style that suits you. You can be an innovator rather than a follower of fashion. Be creative and go for a unique look. Get inspiration by going to jumble sales and second-hand shops. If you're prepared to have a good old rummage and dig deep you can pick up some amazing bargains. Men's blazers and jackets are usually a good find. Antique shops are good places to shop if you like pretty lace dresses and lace blouses. It is important that whatever you choose to wear suits your colouring, personality and figure type. Try some experimenting and you'll be pleased with the results.

Reasons For Looking Good

* By looking good you can boost your confidence and feel ready to take on anything.

* Looking good shows that you are happy with life.

* You will gain respect by dressing in the right clothes for the right occasion.

* You have to present an attractive image for example if you are representing an important company.

* You are more likely to impress other people if you are feeling confident with your appearance.

* If you look good, you will get admiration from people around you making you feel even better.

* Choosing the right clothes can enhance your individuality.

* By taking the way you look into consideration, you will give the impression of being able to consider others.

* Looking good shows that you like yourself. It is much easier for people to like you, when they know that you like yourself.

Chapter Five

accessories

The Importance of Accessories

Accessories play a very important part in fashion. The right accessories can make an outfit, while the wrong ones can ruin a look. They are a way of expressing your individuality, and can change your look from one day to the next depending on the mood you're in. Whether you go for a classic look, or a look of your very own, your accessories will add the finishing touches to your outfit. Try experimenting and decide on what you look best in. It's important that they go with your overall look and fit in with your lifestyle. Make sure that you feel comfortable in what you're wearing and always wear too little rather than too much if you're not sure of the right balance.

Jewellery

Jewellery is great for accessorising and can be used to dress up an outfit. If you were going out straight from work for example, you could put on some earrings, a necklace and a brooch and completely transform your look. It is important that you choose the right jewellery for the right outfit. If you have spent a lot of money on something which looks very smart, then it will obviously need to be accessorised with classy jewellery. The real thing, gold and silver, can be expensive, but if chosen with thought can be worn for years and years without dating. Gold will suit you if you have warm skin tones whereas silver will suit you if you have cool ones.

Make sure that your jewellery complements your size. Large chunky jewellery will look too overpowering on a small person, just the same as tiny pearls or stud earrings will look completely lost on someone with a large build. If you are wearing something very stylish, then keep your jewellery to a minimum, otherwise you will over do things and ruin the look. Brightly coloured junk jewellery looks best worn with casual clothes, adding a splash of colour. Pearl earrings are good for softening a look.

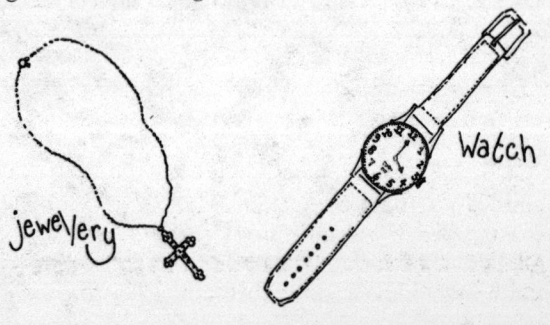

For evenings, go for big bold jewellery. Large hoop earrings look fabulous in gold or silver. Large drop earrings, necklaces and bracelets look wonderful in diamanté and crystal, and are great for special occasions like parties. If you prefer a more individual look, check out your local second-hand shops and antique markets for unusual items. You can find rings, earrings and brooches at real bargain prices.

Watches are an important item of jewellery because they are functional too. There are many different styles to choose from. You can choose a classy watch if you're a classic dresser, in a new modern design, or you could go for one of those watches that looks antique, but is in fact new. They are particularly fashionable at the moment. Real antique watches can be picked up at reasonable prices from antique markets, but they don't usually come with a guarantee. However, I know someone that picked up a beautiful antique watch from a second-hand shop. She got it at a good price and fitted a lovely strap, and was told by the jeweller where she bought the strap that it was 22 carat gold. It keeps the time too! If you dress very casually, then a fun type watch or even two is the answer. Watches have come down in price a lot over the past few years so it isn't extravagant owning more than one. Cheap fun watches are ideal for holidays and many of them are now waterproof too.

Quick Tips

* If you have a short neck go for longer length necklaces and don't wear dangly earrings.

* Wear a necklace in gold and silver if you don't want to be restricted to just one metal for the rest of your jewellery.

* Dress up a boring jacket with an attractive brooch.

* Keep your hands in good condition with well manicured nails if you wear rings because they draw attention to your hands.

* Only wear 'piled' on jewellery if you're wearing a very plain outfit.

Belts

It's a good idea to have a selection of belts to go with different outfits. Belts are functional but they are decorative too. Choose your belts with gold or silver buckles depending on what you wear most. Belts are a good way of giving stunning emphasis on the waist or hips, and they come in an array of materials. You can transform an outfit by changing a cheap belt for a more expensive one with an attractive buckle. Make sure that the belt you wear goes with the fabric of your outfit. Wear classics like snakeskin and leather to go with a smart look. Ethnic styles look best with tough leather, beading, rope, webbing and any other natural fibres. Silks and velvets look best with evening clothes. You can make your own belt by using beads, rope, a scarf or even a chain. For a coordinated look, match your belt to your shoes. Wear a belt in the same colour of your outfit if you don't want to over define the waist area.

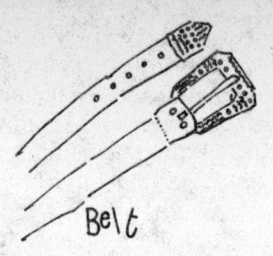

Quick Tips

* If you are small, avoid wide belts in contrasting colours. They will break up your body shape and make you seem smaller.

* Make the most of a small waist by wearing a nice wide fitted belt.

* Avoid tight belts if you're big.

* Never wear a narrow belt through wide loops.

Bags

The bag that you choose will receive a lot of wear and tear so it's an accessory well worth spending money on. Leather is very hard wearing and a lot of people say it improves with age, so it's a good choice. Choose a shape that won't date too quickly and make sure that the colour fits in with your wardrobe. You should take your shape into account too. If you are big you will look ridiculous with a small bag and the same goes for small people with big bags. If you are short and go for a bag with a strap, make sure that the strap is adjustable. Classic dressers should choose sturdy square or rectangular shaped bags. If you go for the casual look you should choose a satchel, duffle bag or canvas bag in a bright colour. People that like a soft pretty look will suit bags in soft fabrics with curved edges and small gathers. Make sure your bag is big enough to fit everything you are likely to need from day to day.

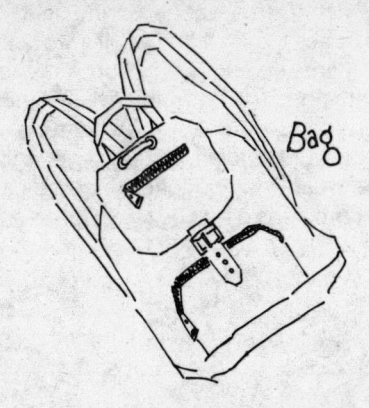

Quick Tips

* Buy the best bag that you can afford and it will be a worthwhile investment.

* Use protective sprays (ozone friendly, of course!) and polish on leather bags.

* Tidy out your bag at least once a week, otherwise it will get full of more and more clutter, weighing you down and making you look unbalanced.

* Try to choose a bag with pockets for your purse and keys. Then you won't be forever hunting at the bottom of your bag, which is where your purse and keys always end up!

* If your bag has a shoulder strap, make sure that it is strong enough for the weight you'll be carrying, otherwise it could snap.

Lingerie

There is an enormous range of lingerie to choose from, from the sexy lacy look to the thermal type of underwear. The important thing is to choose what you feel comfortable in, and make sure that it fits properly. A good outfit can be ruined by ill-fitting undies. Always try on bras, making sure that you have the right cup size and that it is comfortable. Flesh bulging out of cups or under the arms is very unattractive. Make sure that your knickers fit snugly, and if you want to avoid a VPL (Visible Panty Line) when wearing tight fitting clothes, try French knickers or boxer shorts. If you want a smooth line, wear a 'body' which is like a swimsuit, and is very comfortable. 'Bodies' do up under the crotch with poppers, hook and eye fasteners or buttons. Go for a 'body' with poppers because they are far more comfortable, and always make sure that the 'body' is long enough, otherwise it will ride up. Thermal underwear is no longer considered naff. In fact it is quite trendy. Beat the chill and go for cosy long johns and snug vests.

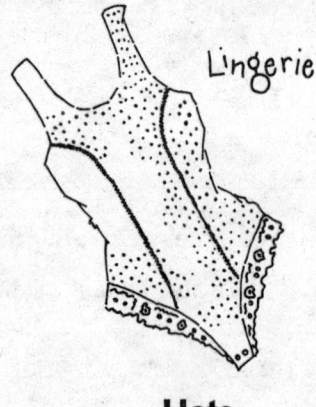

Lingerie

Hats

Hats are gaining popularity again. In the forties most people wouldn't be seen without one. Then the fashion died out and people only wore them for weddings and special occasions. Now people are starting to wear them again and they are considered an important fashion item once more.

When choosing a hat, make sure that it suits your face, figure and lifestyle. It is important that it fits in with the style of your wardrobe. Always check how you look in a full length mirror, and make sure that it is a good fit. If you are small go for something fairly quiet. If you are tall you can be extravagant and wear hats with wide brims. Style your hair in different ways when wearing a hat to see which style looks best. Wear a hat in the winter to keep warm, because most of our body heat is lost through our head. When choosing a hat for a special occasion, make sure the hat shape suits your face but above all, that it goes with your outfit. Take your outfit along with you to the shop if you are unsure. If you buy a designer hat, consider how much wear you will get from it because they can be very pricey.

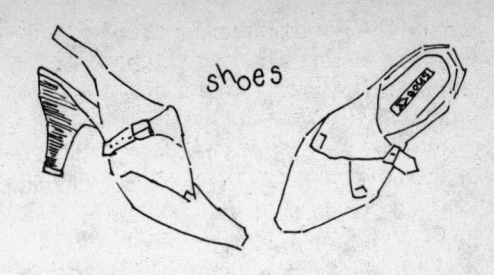

Shoes

When you buy a pair of shoes, make sure that they fit well and that they are comfortable. If they don't feel comfortable you will hardly get any wear from them. If you buy lots of shoes, then you can have a variety of colours and styles to go with different outfits. However, if you only own a couple of pairs, then you are best choosing black and brown – then they will go with most things. Have one casual pair, and one pair for dressier occasions. Brogues, loafers and Doctor Martens are perfect for daywear because they are comfortable and hard wearing. For the evening, choose something a little dressier. Some small heeled slingbacks, lace ups with a Louis heel or a classic pair of black suede pumps or court shoes (not too high) – the choice is yours. Wear canvas shoes or plimsolls in the summer to ring the changes. If you buy a pair of boots, choose a classic style or a style that you won't get bored with. Boots are expensive, so you want to get a couple of seasons wear out of them at least.

Quick Tips

* Make sure you sole and heel your shoes or boots regularly, and they will last much longer. Worn down shoes just give you a terribly scruffy appearance.

* Walk around the shop in a new pair of shoes for a good while before deciding if they are for you.

* If you are small, avoid wearing very high heels.

* If your shoes pinch, fill them with hot water, leave them for a few seconds and pour the water out. Quickly put the shoes on and you will find that the water has softened them, making them stretchable.

Tights

There are more tights on the market to choose from than ever before. There are opaque and woolly tights which are best worn in the winter. There are fishnet and lacy tights which are great for dressy evenings, and there are many types of tights that can be worn in the summer. Sheer tights come in every colour imaginable. There are tights with motifs, patterns, spots and stripes which look great with casual outfits. If you want to draw attention to your legs you have plenty of options, because the list goes on and on. Always carry a spare pair of tights in your bag, just in case you ladder or snag them. Nothing looks worse than holey tights.

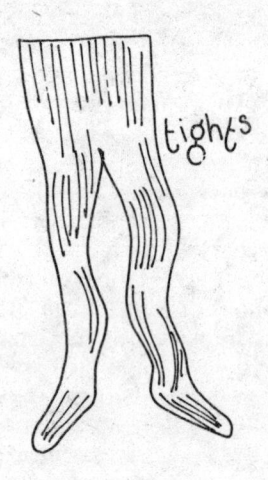

Quick Tips

* Heavy legs should stick to neutrals with toning shoes. If your legs are big, but you like wearing woolly tights, go for the fine woolly kind so they don't make your legs look any bigger.

* Denier is the hosiery term for thickness. The lower the figure, the sheerer the tights.

* Skinny legs look best in thick woolly tights.

* Wash your tights after every wear to keep them fresh and clean and to restore their elasticity.

Umbrellas

Umbrellas are a must in our climate, and there are millions to choose from. If you like to dress in a casual way choose your umbrella in a fun colour, or choose spots, stripes, or even an umbrella with an animal head for a handle. Go for the black collapsible type if you dress more classically. They're good for fitting in your bag, and black makes them look more expensive.

umbrella

Quick Tips

* Go for a manual umbrella rather than an automatic one because they last longer.
* Leave a wet umbrella fully open until it has completely dried out, otherwise it will start to smell stale and awful.

Gloves

Gloves are essential for the cold winter months. Choose woolly mittens or gloves in bright colours for a fun look. Or go for a lovely soft leather pair that come in an array of beautiful colours, for a look of class.

glove

Quick Tips

* Make sure that your gloves fit properly across the knuckles and in the fingers.
* Get rid of dirty marks on leather gloves with a rubber.

Perfume

Perfume should be a daily essential. All women deserve to smell nice and there is no better way of smelling nice than wearing perfume. There are so many perfumes to choose from, so where do you begin? Well the only way to find a perfume that you like is to try out the perfume testers.

Never buy a perfume because you have smelt it on a friend and liked it, because it might smell totally different on you. Never smell perfume just from the bottle either, you have to spray a perfume onto your wrist and wait a couple of minutes to get the full lingering effect. Some people wear different perfumes for different occasions, whereas other people just stick to the one. There are so many fragrances, that it seems a shame not to experiment and choose a different brand occasionally. With perfume you generally find that the most expensive ones smell more pleasant. They are more expensive because they take much longer to produce. With a good perfume, a little goes a long way, so apply in small amounts and re-apply only occasionally.

Quick Tips

* Don't throw away old perfume bottles. Take off the tops and put the empty bottles between your clothes in your drawers.

* Use bath oil, body lotion, and talc in the same fragrance as your perfume, for a longer lasting aroma.

* Apply perfume to your pulse points (the inner wrist, the crook of the elbow, the throat and the back of the knee) which being your body hot spots will make your perfume last much longer.

* Always replace the lid on your perfume, otherwise it will evaporate.

* Keep perfume in its box, or in a cool dark place. Light can cause a chemical reaction and change the nature of the perfume.

* If you have sensitive skin, avoid wearing perfume. Spray your pillow, fabric clothes hangers if you have any, and even your ironing board before ironing, to give yourself a pleasant aroma.

Chapter Six

Make-up

The Importance of Make-Up

Make-up is a very important part of looking good. You can have the most amazing outfit on but if your make-up isn't up to scratch you might as well not bother. Today there are so many different types of make-up to choose from, from the very expensive brands to the cheap and cheerful. The more expensive brands usually have much better packaging, a wider choice of colours and are usually not so perfumed. However, some people swear by their cheaper brands, so really your make-up is an individual thing depending on what suits you. I do think that it is worth paying out for a good foundation however, and many professional make-up artists would agree with me. Having a good base is one of the most important parts of making up. A smooth base is like a blank canvas for you to create a look that suits you, so it needs to be the right colour and texture.

Foundation

You should choose a foundation closest to your skin tone. If you have pale skin, don't try to make it look darker with a dark foundation because this will just look really unnatural. Also bear in mind that your skin tone can change colour. In the summer if you get a suntan you will probably need a darker foundation. If your skin is pale go for an ivory foundation. If you have creamy skin you need a foundation in bisque or golden beige. Medium tone beige skin suits many shades, choose beige, golden and suntan tones. Olive skins suit golden colours with a touch of rose, while darker skins suit brown earthy foundations.

If you can't find a foundation that suits your skin tone, try mixing two together for a perfect match. Some people find foundation a little too heavy to wear during the day. If you're one of these people, try adding a touch of moisturiser to your foundation to make a lighter base, or go for a tinted moisturiser instead. You can choose your foundation to match your skin type as well as your skin tone. There are matt foundations which are great for greasy skin, or if you're prone to spots try a medicated foundation. Dry skins should use foundation creams or stick foundations which contain moisturising ingredients. Liquid foundations tend to be lighter and suit most skin types.

Foundation should only be applied to clean moisturised skin. It should never be applied over stale make-up. Use your fingertips and dot the foundation over the central areas of your face. Then using a damp sponge give a nice even coverage, working from the centre of the face outwards. Take your time blending your foundation and make sure that there aren't any tide marks. Blend your foundation over your eyelids and around your neck getting into all the crevices with a sponge and finish off by smoothing with your fingertips. Make sure that you use your foundation sparingly – you don't want it to look caked on.

Quick Tips

* If you have dark shadows under your eyes, use a concealer or a lighter coloured foundation that you can blend until it merges with your make-up base.

* If you have skin blemishes, use an opaque cover up that matches the shade of your foundation.

* Minimise facial faults with shading, using a darker foundation to make a feature recede, and a lighter one to emphasise your best features.

* Slim down a wide nose by blending a darker shade of foundation down each side of the nose, starting from the eyebrows to the nostrils, blending outwards and using a sponge.

* Make a long nose look shorter by blending a darker foundation around the nostrils and under the tip of the nose.

* Minimise a heavy jawline or prominent chin by using a darker foundation, shading the outer edges and blending into the neck.

* Minimise a double chin by using a lighter foundation on the pad of your chin, making it more prominent.

Blusher

Is blusher really necessary and does it improve our looks? Blusher is used for adding colour and warmth to a face. Just a hint of colour on your face can contour your cheeks enhancing your looks. You don't have to wear it, but it is a good way of looking healthy, and if worn correctly it can even improve your face shape.

There are two types of blushers, being a cream blusher or a powder blusher. The powder version is the most common and usually comes in a compact with its own little brush. It is advisable however, to buy a good blusher brush because the ones that come with blushers are usually quite bad in quality and are rough on the face. A nice big soft, good quality brush is best. Powder blushers are also easier to apply than creams because they are easier to control. However, cream blushers have their good points too. They are very good if you suffer from dry skin because they can add moisture as well as colour to the face. They are also good if you just want a natural sheen. Blushers come in shades of peach, tan and pink. You should choose a shade depending on your skin tone, remembering that the softer your colouring the softer the shade of blusher you should wear.

Blusher is meant to be a subtle colour enhancing your face. Don't make the mistake so many people make by having a hard wedge of colour because it looks awful. It is much better to start with a little blusher, adding more until you get the right strength. If you use too much blusher, you'll find that having to remove it will prove messy and difficult. Powder blusher should be applied after your foundation and face powder. Put a little blusher on your brush, always tapping the brush to get rid of any surplus powder. Suck in your cheeks and brush up and out from the hollow of your cheeks to your temples. Cream blusher should be applied after your foundation but before your face powder. You can use your fingertips or a sponge, blending up and outwards to the temple, making sure that there are no patches of colour.

Quick Tips

* Wear a blusher that complements your lipstick.

* For daywear try a matt blusher in a natural shade.

* Make a long face look shorter with a triangle of colour.

* Use a highlighter (a lighter coloured blusher) to accentuate the angles and bones of your face. Concentrate on your upper cheeks, blending it with your blusher giving your face a radiant look.

* Try a frosted blusher for evening wear.

* Wear a golden blusher with a tan.

* When applying blusher be sure to blend away any harsh edges. Make sure your blusher is barely noticeable from the side of your face. There should be no streaks.

* Narrow a square jawline, and make your face look slimmer with a crescent of colour.

Face Powder

Face powder is applied after your foundation. It helps to set your make-up, giving a nice smooth even finish to your complexion with a sheen or matt look. It also covers the shine from oil prone areas of your face, particularly the forehead and centre panel. If you wear cream eyeshadows or eye pencils, powder is a necessity to stop any ugly creases forming. By wearing face powder your make-up has more staying power.

There are two different types of face powder to choose from. Loose powder, which is best for the final finish to your make-up. Or pressed powder, which comes in a compact, and is very convenient for re-touching make-up during the day. A fine, loose, translucent, colourless powder is best for a soft natural look. Translucent powders slightly affect other make-up colours, whereas coloured powders can make a major difference. You can get face powders in shades of pink, brown and golden tones. If you use a coloured powder, always choose it one shade lighter than your foundation.

Apply your face powder after your foundation, and any other cream-based cosmetics that you may use, and before any powder eyeshadows or blushers. Using a powder puff, take a generous amount of powder, and starting at the neck and chin apply upwards with gentle press and turn motions. Concentrate on one small area at a time paying particular attention to the central areas of your face. Cover your entire face including your eyelids, and using a large powder brush, brush or whisk away any excess powder with downward strokes. This prevents any powder from getting caught in facial hairs, or settling into fine lines around the eyes. Powder should be like an invisible film. Check that it is well blended over your face and that there are no shiny areas or caked patches, especially around the chin and nostrils.

Quick Tips

* If using a pressed powder from a compact, be careful not to apply too many layers, otherwise it will look caked on.

* Remember that translucent powder makes your foundation a fraction lighter.

* You can now buy a compact make-up which contains both foundation and powder all in one. It is very convenient for quick repairs during the day, and is much handier for carrying around in your bag.

Eye Shadow

Your eyes are probably the most noticeable feature on your face, and make-up can work wonders. With careful shading you can add colour and dimension, but it is important that you get your beauty sleep. Otherwise, instead of having healthy and sparkling eyes, they will look puffy and bloodshot. With some simple eyecare and a bit of creation you can set off the colour and shape of your eyes, improving your overall appearance.

Many people make the common mistake of matching their eyeshadow to their outfit or eyes. The results can be disastrous. Choose colours according to your skin tone, bearing in mind that darker colours contour the eyes intensifying their shape, while paler colours are best as highlighters. Eye Shadows come in different variations so it is up to you to choose what suits you best. Eye Shadow creams are oil based and can be applied with a brush or fingertips. They are easy to blend and should be set with powder. Powders are compressed and have an added moisturiser to give cling. They can be applied with a sponge applicator or brush and have good staying power. Crayons and pencils are very waxy and soft. They are easy to apply and don't pull or drag the skin. Colour is drawn on and then blended with the fingertips.

Cover your eyelids and browbone with a light shade blending your eye shadow up and out. Blend a darker colour on your eyelids working from the inside corner of your eye. If you want to change the shape of your eyes, you can do so with some skilful shading:

Droopy Eyelids: Apply your eye shadow in upswept movements onto the browbone concentrating colour on your eyelid. Pencil the inner rim of your eye in white or a very pale colour.

Narrow Eyelids: Use a very pale colour all over your eyelid using a deeper colour in the socket line. Take the colour under your eye and fade onto your browbone.

Small Eyes: Pluck your eyebrows to give yourself maximum eye area. Blend a little pale eye shadow onto your eyelids and then onto your browbone. Apply a deep colour in your eye socket winging it out at the sides, and taking the colour under your lower lashes. Use mascara applying more to your upper lashes.

Quick Tips

* Always blend your eye shadow so there are no visible hard lines between the shades.

* Don't forget to use brushes and sponge applicators to reach the corners that fingers can't. Good quality sable brushes are best for blending.

* Keep your applicators and brushes clean. Dirty brushes can cause eye infections.

* Use powder eye shadow for staying power. It is also less likely to crease.

* Don't restrict yourself to just one colour. Blend two or even three shades for a stunning look.

* Keep eye pencils sharp for easier control and application.

* Don't keep pencils in a warm place or in direct sunlight, they will go soft and gooey, or even melt. Put pencils in your fridge to harden before sharpening.

* Go for matt eye shadows for daytime and frosted ones for evening when the light is dimmer.

* Test eye shadows on the back of your hand.

* When applying your eye shadow, place a tissue under your lower lashes to catch any loose powder.

Mascara

Mascara emphasises your eyes and adds the final touch to your eye make-up. Usually it comes in a small wand applicator with a brush. There are different sized brushes to choose from. Some have extra fibres which thicken and lengthen your lashes, and some are thick whilst others are thin. You have to experiment with them to see which suits you most. There are also waterproof and non-waterproof mascaras. If you're going to a wedding or to see a sad film, or even swimming, make sure that you wear a waterproof mascara to avoid black streaks down your face. Coloured mascaras can look great on their own without wearing eye shadow, especially if they tone with your eye colouring. They look brilliant with a suntan too. Go for soft colours if you're blonde or fair skinned, and dark dramatic colours if you're brunette or have a dark skin colouring.

To apply it, start at the root of your eyelashes and work to the tips. Coat both top and bottom lashes, giving two or three coats. Allow mascara to dry between each coat. Make sure the mascara doesn't clog or look lumpy.

Quick Tips

* Use an eyelash curler before applying mascara. It will make your lashes look longer and curlier.

* Remember that two or three light coats of mascara are better than one heavy one.

* For a natural look separate lashes with a lash comb.

* Try to choose a mascara that can be removed easily. Or if not, make sure that you have a good eye make-up remover because the skin around the eyes is very delicate.

* Remove any mascara smudges with a cotton bud. They're great for removing any make-up mistakes.

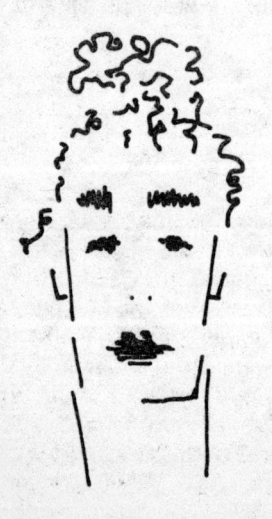

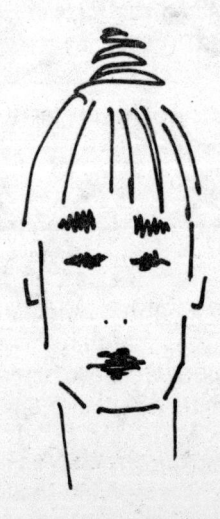

Lipstick

Lips look best with shine and colour. Wearing lipstick adds colour to your face giving you a feminine touch.

There are lots of types to choose from. Lipliner pencils are soft wax based crayons, used to outline the lips. Lip pencils, which can outline and fill in the lips. Lip gloss, which contains glycerine, is usually clear and colourless, and gives the lips shine, and lipsticks, which are the most common of all, being colours and oils dispersed in a wax base with added lanolin for softness. Lipsticks can be applied direct, but for best results should be applied with a lip brush. It is important that your lip colour complements your natural skin tone. Fair haired and fair skinned people should stick to peach, coral or pink shades while dark haired, dark skinned people look best in shades of red, plum or burgundy.

Before applying your lipstick put foundation on your lips and dust with powder. This acts as a base making your lipstick stay on longer. You will also find it easier to apply. Outline your lips with a lip pencil, making sure that the lip pencil is nice and sharp, and that it is a similar match to your lipstick. Start the outline on your bottom lip, outlining from the centre of your mouth to the corners, and then do the same for your top lip. The lipliner pencil will help to prevent your lipstick from bleeding. Now fill in your lips by using a good quality lip brush, starting at the centre and working outwards. You will have more control using a lip brush and get better results. Also your lipstick will have more staying power. Finally, blot your lips with a tissue and add more lip colour.

If you're not happy with the shape of your lips, with a little skill and know how you can change their shape. Here's how:

Full Lips: Apply your lipliner pencil just inside your natural lip line and avoid colours that are bright, heavy or shiny. Stick to light shades instead.

Thin Lips: Apply your lipliner pencil just outside your natural lip line and fill in with a deep colour.

Uneven Lips: Balance out the shape of your lips by applying your lipliner pencil just inside or outside your natural lip line. Fill in with two slightly different shades, using a dark shade for the thickest lip and a lighter shade for the other.

Shapeless Lips: With your lipliner pencil draw in a good shape and fill in with a medium shade lipstick.

Big Lips: Apply your lipliner pencil just inside your natural lip line and fill in with a light shade lipstick.

Quick Tips

* Use vaseline instead of a lip gloss. It's cheap and will keep your lips in good condition.

* If you haven't got a very steady hand rest your elbow on a hard surface while you draw your lip line.

* If you wear bright shades of lipstick, look after your teeth because you'll be drawing attention to them.

* Keep your lipsticks away from sunlight otherwise they will melt.

* Remember that some shades of lipstick, especially dark shades, can stain the lips.

* If you haven't got the time to apply your lipstick with a lip brush, wear lip gloss instead, or try using a lip pencil. Lip pencils are quick and easy to apply.

* If you're bored with your lip colours, try mixing two tones together for a different shade.

* Always re-apply lipstick after eating a meal or drinking.

Eyeliner

Eyeliner helps to define the shape of the eye. You need a steady hand, time and patience to apply a delicate line.

Liquid eyeliner is oil based in water, it comes in a multitude of colours and is applied with a fine brush. It can be quite difficult to control. Cake eyeliner is a coloured powder which is used with water. It is one of the best forms of eyeliner, and is applied by dampening the powder and applying with a fine brush. It tends to be a bit gooey and you have to allow time for it to dry, otherwise it will smudge. An eyeliner pen gives more precision and is good if you're short of time because it's easy to control. Eye pencils can be used as eyeliners. They give a softer line, looking more natural.

Apply your eyeliner with a very fine tipped brush. Support your elbow on a flat surface to give yourself a steady hand. Work from the centre of the eye to the outer corner, keeping the line as close to the lashes as possible.

Quick Tips

* If you use eye pencils, make sure that they're soft otherwise they will drag the skin.

* Coloured kohl pencil can look really stunning worn inside the lower lash line, especially if you choose a shade which reflects your eye colour.

* To make your eyes look wider, apply a white kohl pencil inside the lower lash line.

* Wear liquid eyeliner if you want a sharp line.

* If you want a more subtle line wear pencils or cake eyeliner, and smudge so that it blends with your lashes and eye shadow.

Looking After Your Eyebrows

Eyebrows make the perfect frame for your eyes, giving expression and balance to your features. They require grooming and definition, so do tidy up straggly brows but avoid any drastic re-shaping. Brush your eyebrows into shape, brushing them up and across. Tweeze them into shape by using short quick movements in the direction of the hair growth. Always pluck eyebrows from underneath, never above. Make it easier by pulling your skin taut and gripping each hair as close to the root as possible.

Your eyebrows start at a point above the inside corner of the eye. The highest point of your eyebrows is directly above the iris. Imagine a straight line from your nostril to the outer corner of the eye. Where this line touches your eyebrows is where your eyebrows should finish. Some eyebrows are thin or fair and look better when they are filled in. If so, use a soft eye pencil, making sure that it is sharp, and apply using short diagonal strokes. Apply colour going against the direction of growth because this looks more subtle than following the hair direction. You can also fill in using an eyebrow powder. This should be applied with a fine brush with a slanted edge. Apply with feathery strokes, using a shade lighter than your own colour, because colour always looks darker on the eyebrows. Finish off by brushing your eyebrows through with a clean brush.

Some Practical Advice

* Always be prepared to try out new colours and ideas, but not just before going out in case you don't like the results.

* Read beauty articles in magazines. They give interesting tips and fill you in on what's new. After all, there's no point in dressing well if your make-up makes you look as if you've been in a time warp. *Remember that like fashion, make-up changes.*

* Apply your make-up in a room with good daylight, or if it is artificial light make sure it is even.

* Keep make-up natural during the day and go for heavier and more shimmery colours at night.

* Always apply too little rather than too much make-up. It is easy to apply more, but harder to remove too much.

* Use a magnifying mirror for best results.

* Always use make-up brushes or applicators when applying make-up. It will go on better and is economical too. By using a lip brush you can use up every last bit of that lipstick.

* Never go to bed with your make-up on no matter how late it is or how tired you are. Always use a good make-up remover. *Remember: cleanse, tone and moisturise every night.*

Chapter Seven

Your Holiday Wardrobe

Tips For Packing

The time has come. The holiday that you've saved all year for is nearly here, and you have to pack. So what do you take on your hols? Far too much probably! No doubt you'll bring half of it back unworn and full of creases, so it will need ironing all over again. But this need not be. Just a little bit of thought is all it takes to make packing easy and pleasurable. First of all, if you're visiting a country that you've never visited before, ask your travel agent about the climate. You can usually find out the daytime temperatures by looking in your brochure, but they don't tell you what it will be like at night. Knowing roughly the average evening temperature will be very useful for packing your night-time clothes.

Get yourself a travel guide and read up on the country that you'll be visiting. If you know a bit about where you're going, it will help you to decide what to pack. Once you know something about the place you're staying at, you'll have a rough idea what type of holiday yours will be. If it's just a sunbathing holiday you'll need to take next to nothing. Whereas if a bit of sightseeing is involved you'll need to pack more clothes for during the day. Buy yourself a cheap purse so that you can take your English money in one, and your foreign currency in the other, without getting your money mixed up.

If you take a travel iron and hair dryer abroad, don't forget that you'll need an adaptor plug. If you don't want to do any ironing when you get to your destination, you have to pack very carefully. As you fold each garment to pack it, slip some tissue paper between each fold. This stops the garment from creasing, because tissue helps to retain air which is the vital ingredient for keeping clothes uncreased. Stuff shoulders with tissue so that they don't get flattened, and slide special garments into polythene bags. The air trapped in the bag stops the garment from being too squashed, and you'll find your clothes will come out as crease free as they went in.

Pack shoes around the edge of your case in shoe bags, or if you haven't got any, plastic bags will do. Packing a pleated skirt can be a nightmare. Using hair grips or paper clips, slip them over the hem of each pleat and the pleats will be held in place. Most suitcases look the same when going around a conveyor belt at the airport. Make yours instantly recognisable in some way. Put a sticker, or some tape on it and you will save yourself time.

What Clothes To Take

When you pack for your holiday try to stick to a basic colour scheme. Take items that can be multi-purpose. Baggy shorts are ideal because they can be worn to the beach and they also look smart for evening. Cotton vests are very useful. You can wear one rolled up during the day and roll it down at night, great to show off those tanned arms. Swimsuits and bikini tops are multi purpose too. A bikini top looks great worn under a knotted chambray shirt. The same goes for swimsuits. They make perfect tops for evening wear, looking good with most things.

Before you pack, lay all your clothes out and check that they can all be mixed and matched. If there is anything that can't be, don't take it. T-shirts are great to take because cotton jersey is ideal for rolling up and stays crease free, filling up the little spaces in your case. Always take a hat if you're going to a very warm climate because hats are a great protection. The sun can be very harmful. Sunstroke is very nasty and could ruin your holiday. A good pair of sunglasses are a must too. The sun's rays can be damaging to the eyes if your eyes aren't protected from it. Cheaper sunglasses don't really cut out the harmful rays, so go for the best you can afford. Beach shoes can be bought on holiday. Most sunny beach resorts have a selection of pumps and espadrills which are really cheap. So cheap, that you can usually wear them out and leave them behind. Make the most of getting a tan and wear clothes with cutaway sections and dresses that have very low backs. Never take a lot of jewellery on holiday. You won't wear it during the day if it's hot, because it will be too uncomfortable. Beware of watch strap marks, they can look very unattractive, and never wear metal in the sun. It acts as a conductor for the heat and can burn the skin.

Remember to take some washing detergent with you. You can now buy it in convenient travel packs. Or buy a small packet when you arrive. It's handy for rinsing out your swimwear and washing small garments.

What Swimsuit?

If you've got big hips go for a medium colour bikini with a halter neck top. Halter neck straplines give the illusion of wider shoulders, balancing the body. If you've got short legs wear a swimsuit or bikini that is cut very highly on the legs – it will make your legs look longer. If you are slim you can go for more elaborate details on a swimsuit or bikini. If you're big it might not be so easy to carry it off. Never wear a bandeau bikini if you have big boobs – you'll look like a sack of potatoes. Make sure that your swimsuit or bikini fits properly. Nothing looks worse than straps digging in, especially if there's some spare flesh hanging over the top. If you're big, you'll look better in an all in one rather than a two piece. Remember that horizontal stripes add width and curve to the body whereas vertical stripes can make you look taller and slimmer.

What To Travel In

Wear something comfortable when travelling to your holiday destination. Travelling usually means lots of sitting around, so something casual is best. If you're travelling to a warmer climate there's no need to wear a coat. It won't be worn for the rest of the holiday and it will probably be too bulky to pack when coming home. Bear in mind that you'll have more in your case when you return, because of your holiday gifts and any duty frees. Jeans are probably the best thing to travel in because they don't crease. Wear a T-shirt, cardigan and lightweight jacket. Layers are better than a heavy jumper and jacket. If you're flying you'll be grateful of the cardigan as you'll find it a bit chilly on the plane because of the air conditioning. When you get to your destination, if it is hot you can peel off your layers and wear your cool T-shirt.

Go for dark colours rather than pale, because you tend to get very grubby whilst travelling. Wear comfortable fitting shoes on the plane because your feet tend to swell up.

Your skin dehydrates when flying and can feel uncomfortable and tight. So take a spray can of water with you and spray your face to freshen yourself up and always carry your toothbrush and toothpaste in your hand luggage. There's nothing worse than having a stale taste in your mouth. If you are a vegetarian get your travel agent to tell the airline before you fly. Then they can have a special vegetarian meal prepared for you. If your flight's a long one, you'll feel better if you don't drink alcohol. Keep your blood sugar level up by drinking lots of water and eating fruit.

Travelling Light

You're going on an island hopping holiday. It's not practical to take a suitcase because of all the travelling around. But how are you going to fit everything into a small holdall? The answer is simple. Believe it or not, with a little careful planning, you can have a brilliant week in the sun by taking just ten items of clothing. The important thing to make this work is to keep the colours to a minimum, making sure they can all be mixed and matched in several ways. I've chosen black, white, bright pink and faded denim, but you can choose different colours if you wish:

1. **Black swimsuit** – can also be worn as a top.

2. **Bright pink cropped vest or bustier top** – good for day or night.
3. **Faded denim jacket**.
4. **Faded denim cut-offs** – can be worn just above the knee, or rolled up to make them shorter.
5. **Baggy white shorts** – good for day or night.
6. **Black slip-on plimsolls** – ideal for holidays.
7. **Bright pink lycra T-shirt dress** – can be worn ruched or straight, very versatile.

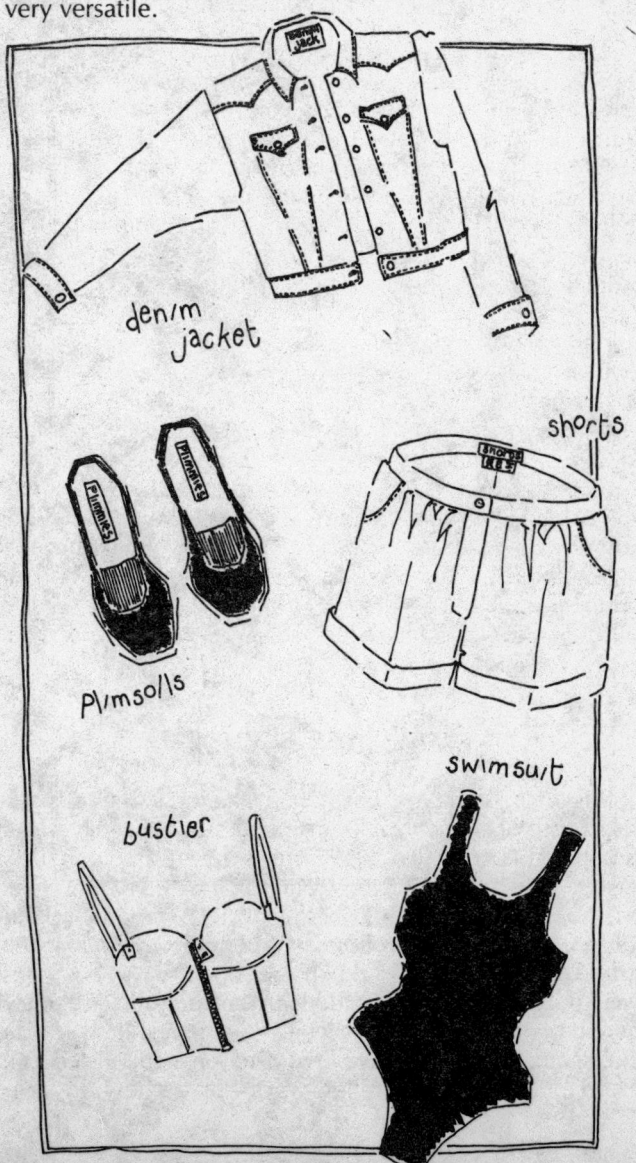

8. **Loose fitting lightweight trousers** – perfect for a smart evening.
9. **Straw hat** – a necessity if it's sunny.
10. **Short denim skirt or black tube skirt** – easy to pack and stylish too. To make your luggage even lighter, you could wear the hat and denim jacket for travelling. The ten items listed can be mixed and matched in endless ways – here's how:

1. **The black swimsuit** can be worn to the beach, but it also looks great worn as a top. Team it with the denim cut-offs, the white shorts, the loose fitting trousers or the short skirt.

swimsuit
+
cut-offs
+
plimsolls

2. **The bright pink top** is perfect for day or evening wear. Team it with the denim cut-offs, the baggy white shorts, the loose fitting trousers or the short skirt.

bustier + denim skirt + plimsolls

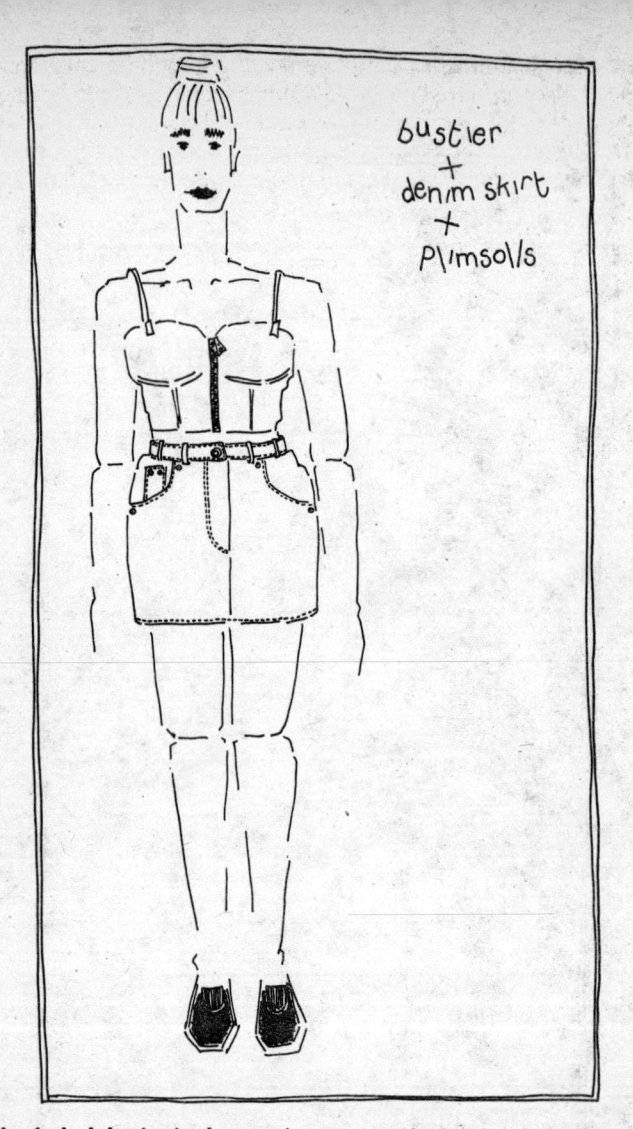

3. **The faded denim jacket** can be worn with absolutely everything.
4. **The faded denim cut-offs** are ideal rolled up short for the beach. Or worn longer for the evening. Team them with the black swimsuit, the bright pink top or the T-shirt dress, worn tucked in as a vest.
5. **The baggy white shorts** are perfect for day or evening wear. Team them with the black swimsuit, the bright pink vest or the T-shirt dress, worn tucked in as a vest.

6. **The black slip-on plimsolls** team well with all the garments.
7. **The T-shirt dress** is another garment that is perfect for day or evening wear. Team it with the faded denim cut-offs, the baggy white shorts, the loose fitting trousers (worn over the trousers and ruched up), the short skirt (tucked into the denim one, and ruched over the tube one).

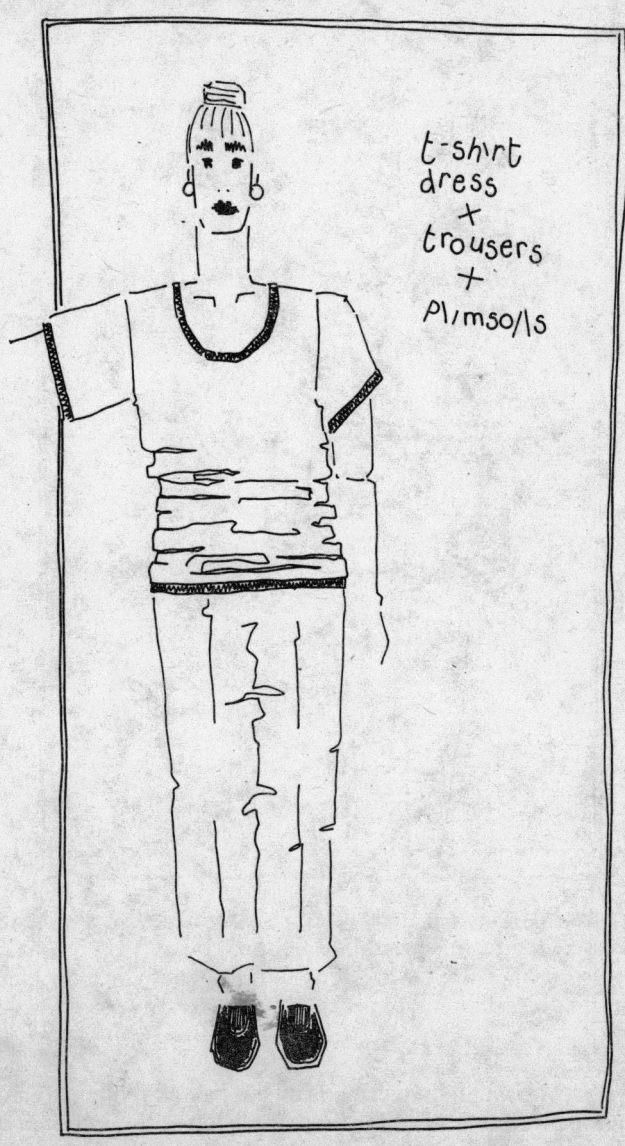

t-shirt dress + trousers + plimsolls

8. **The loose fitting trousers** are for evening wear only. Team them with the black swimsuit, the bright pink top or the T-shirt dress.
9. **The straw hat** will go with all of the looks.

denim jacket
×
shorts
×
plimsolls
×
straw hat

10. **The short skirt** can be worn during the day or at night. Team it with the black swimsuit, the bright pink top or the T-shirt dress.

t-shirt
dress
+
denim skirt
+
plimsolls

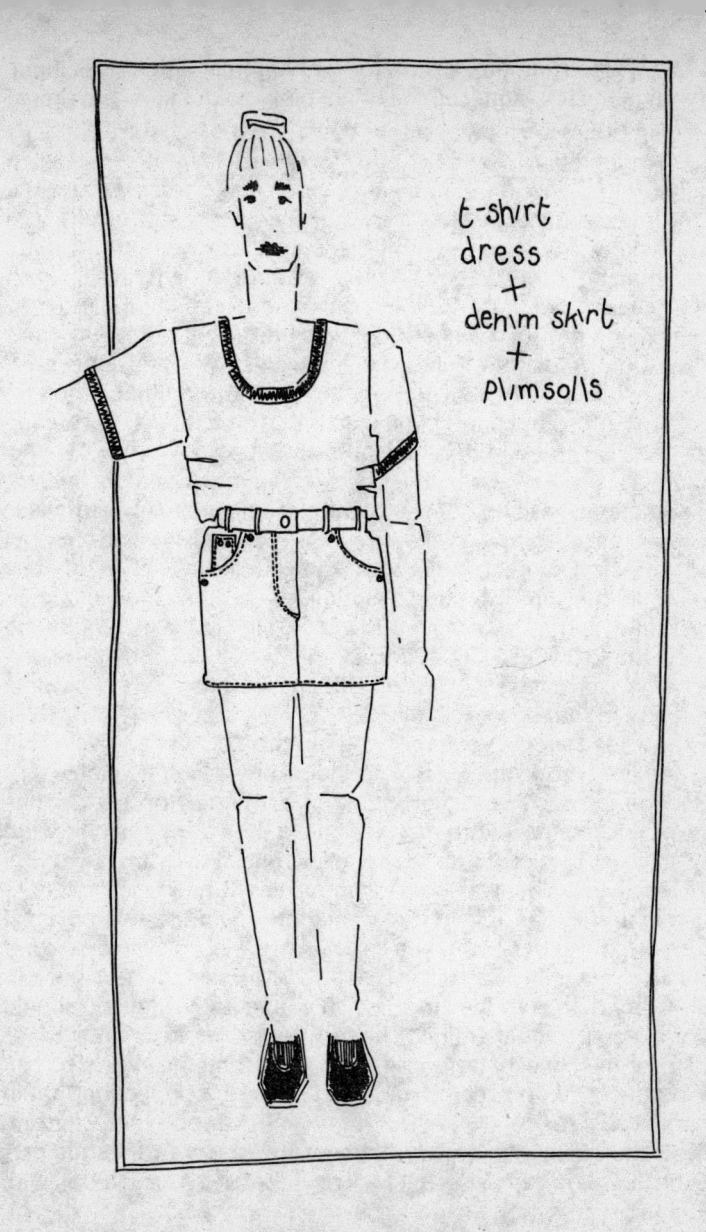

Your Skin In The Sun

Everybody loves to get a suntan. It makes you look and feel incredibly healthy. It can put glowing highlights in your hair, and make your eyes seem clearer and your teeth whiter. The sun is good for you to a certain extent. It formulates vitamin D in the skin, which is essential for strong bones and growth. However, like most things, it is only good in moderation. Too much sun can be very harmful. There are a variety of suntan lotions and creams which make tanning safer, but people do tend to be a bit careless when it comes to sunbathing. We go a bit potty when we see a bit of sun because we don't live in a sunny climate. A lobster body is quite a common sight on a Spanish beach, because we head for the beach ignoring all the rules.

The reason the sun can be harmful is because it contains potentially harmful radiation, otherwise known as UVA and UVB rays. Only five to ten per cent of the sun's rays are absorbed into the skin which doesn't sound a lot, but the cells that are endangered are the ones that give the skin its suppleness and elasticity, so this is why sunburn occurs. The warning signs are reddening of the skin, itching, and sometimes swelling and blistering. Too much sun can cause sunstroke affecting the skin's sweating mechanism, and causing headaches and nausea. To get a safe tan you mustn't spend too long too soon in the sun. By taking it gradually you allow the melanin in your skin to build up. Melanin is a dark pigment which is in and around the growing layer of our skin. It's the skin's own natural defence system, and it screens out the harmful rays providing protection in the form of a suntan.

So how long should you stay in the sun? It all depends on your skin type and how strong the sun is. You should buy a suntan lotion with a protection factor. The higher the SPF (Sun Protection Factor), the more protection the lotion will give you. A fair skinned person should only stay out in the sun for ten minutes, but by wearing an SPF of eight, she will probably be safe for about eighty minutes. Eight times longer than she'd be able to survive without any protection cream at all. If you have darker skin, you can probably get away with a lower protection factor and stay out in the sun a bit longer. The skin on your face is very delicate. Therefore, when you're in the sun you should pay it extra special attention. The most sensitive areas on the face tend to be the cheekbones, nose, lips and around the eyes. You can buy products that prevent dryness and give extra protection, but in my opinion, a sun block is best. This comes in a solid stick form and cuts out most of the sun's rays. Other sensitive areas are the shoulders and the feet. You can use a sunblock on these, or a suntan lotion with a very high protection factor.

It is important that you look after your skin before you go on holiday, and also while you are on holiday. Before you go you could use a pre-tanning lotion. These moisturise your skin making it smooth and supple, but also claim to stimulate the melanin production in the skin so that you tan easier and faster. However, they are rather expensive, so if your budget doesn't run to it, use a simple body lotion instead. Body lotions do the same job as aftersun lotions, and you will find that they are much cheaper, sometimes half the price. If your skin is well moisturised before and during your holiday, it will soak up the sun and you will keep your tan longer. After spending time in the sun you should take a shower, removing all the suntan lotion and unblocking your pores. Then smother yourself all over in body lotion. Do this after your holiday too, to prolong your tan when the sun has long gone. By following these simple instructions you should tan without tears and have fun in the sun.

Your Hair In The Sun

Your hair needs just as much protection from the sun as your skin does. After all, if you're going to the trouble of getting a healthy tan, you don't want your hair to let you down. The sun isn't the only thing on holiday that is damaging to your hair. The sea is very harmful because it is so salty. The sand which is gritty gets into the scalp, there's the chlorine in swimming pools and even the breeze from the sea can be damaging, making your hair knotty. Most people find that their hair gets very dry because of all of these things. If your hair is bleached or permed, then you are even more vulnerable. Extra care has to be taken so that your hair doesn't weaken. Follow these simple guidelines to keep your hair from looking dull and damaged. Make it shiny and healthy instead, to go with your tan.

Start off on the right foot by having a good cut and conditioning treatment before your holiday, getting rid of all those split ends. Protect your hair by wearing a hat or scarf as often as you can when you're in direct sunlight. If you don't like wearing hats, wear a hair gel instead which will act as a protection against the harmful ultra violet rays. If you do a lot of swimming it's a good idea to rub lots of conditioner into your hair. Then when you've had your swim, rinse your hair in clean water and apply more conditioner. Brush your hair through using a pure bristle brush. Make sure you brush gently, because you can damage your hair when it's wet, by tearing it and causing split ends. If it's breezy, wear a hat or scarf, otherwise your hair will get really knotty. Having to brush out knots can be a real pain, and can also cause your hair to tear giving you split ends.

At the end of your day, give your hair a good wash. If you haven't been swimming there'll probably be bits of sand in it, so wash it anyway. Use loads of conditioner and leave it on for about five minutes so it really gets to work. Try not to use a hairdryer on your hair unless you really have to. Hairdryers are damaging at the best of times, and even more so if you've been in the sun. Let your hair dry naturally instead. If you don't like the natural look, experiment with hair accessories. Put your hair up using a covered band (never an elastic one) or experiment with hair combs, slides, clips or hairbands. You'll be amazed at the looks you can achieve. If you want curls, use bendy rods instead of heated rollers or tongs, they're less damaging.

Quick Tips

* Don't take white stilettos with you on holiday just because they'll go with everything you've packed. Take white pumps instead, they're less common and tarty.

* If you're going on holiday with your boyfriend, don't let him wear socks and trainers with his shorts. It looks so British and naff.

* Get a bikini with a back fastener. Then when you tan your back, you can undo the back, and not get ugly strap marks.

* Carry a small amount of foreign currency as well as your travellers cheques. If your plane is delayed, the banks and hotel cashiers could be closed, spelling disaster.

* Always take headache tablets and tablets for an upset stomach. Medicine can be terribly expensive abroad.

* Always drink bottled water, just to be on the safe side.

* Take a Walkman, they're great for the beach.

* Make a holiday list and cross the items off as you pack them.

* If you're going to call home while you're away, try to find out the correct code before you go. It could save you time and confusion.

* Never get so carried away with having a great holiday that you travel home in your beach shorts. The weather here will be freezing and you'll look an idiot.

* Build a suntan up gradually if you want it to last. If you try to tan too quickly you'll burn and peel, making your tan look patchy.

* Take a selection of different shaped swimsuits and bikinis. By alternating them you'll get rid of ugly strap marks.

* Don't make the mistake of thinking you can't burn if it's cloudy. The sun's rays are more powerful than you think.

* Never sunbathe between twelve and three o'clock. The sun is at its most dangerous because it is at its highest. Therefore, there are less ozone layers for it to penetrate through.

* Take a container of moist tissues. They're handy for travelling and if you have snacks on the beach.

* Wear a good pair of sunglasses to reduce ultra violet light. It can be damaging to your eyes and can give you headaches.

* Take a dual purpose holdall that can be your beach bag as well.

* If you have sensitive skin, don't wear perfume in the sun. You could cause a skin reaction that the sun would aggravate.

* Stuff your socks into your shoes. It saves space and helps your shoes keep their shape.

* Don't spend lots of time in the water thinking that the sun can't harm you, because it can. Wear a water resistant suntan lotion.

* Take a lightweight beach robe that can combine as a dressing gown.

* Pack some pegs – it saves your bikini from ending up on the balcony downstairs.

* If you're on a boat or in an open top car, don't let the cooling breeze fool you. The sun is probably just as powerful, so be cautious.

* Apply your suntan lotion before you step outside. If it's very sunny, you could burn just by walking to the beach.

* If there's just two of you, invest in a camera with an automatic timer, for hours of fun.

* Take a packet of sweets for your flight. They stop your ears from popping *and* they taste nice!

* If you're blonde, squeeze lemon on your hair and the sun will bring out your natural highlights.

* Take some extra money with you if going abroad, so you can treat yourself. You can sometimes pick up great bargains. In Spain for example, you can get wonderful leather items such as purses, bags and shoes at bargain prices.

* Take a good Swiss Army knife with you on holiday. They contain everything from a bottle opener to eyebrow tweezers and prove very useful.

* Lastly, never buy a Spanish donkey. You'll lose every bit of cool that you have.

Chapter Eight

Glasses

Wearing glasses doesn't mean that you have to lack style. Believe it or not, twenty-four million of us need help with our eyesight, so if you have to wear glasses don't feel like giving up on your appearance. Follow these simple guidelines instead and look 'spectacular'.

Where To Get Your Eyes Tested

If you think that you may need glasses it's important that you go for an eye test. Ask a friend to recommend an optician. If not you can get a list of qualified opticians which is compiled by your area family practitioner. The list is kept in libraries and main Post Offices. Look for a 'QO' sign (Qualified Optician) outside a practice.

The Eye Test

The Optometrist will make checks on your vision, and if it needs correcting he will discuss this with you and give you a written prescription. Once you have been given the prescription, the choice is yours. You can either have it dispensed at the practice where you've had your eyes examined, or you can shop around, if they don't have any frames that you particularly like. Once you choose your frames and lenses ask the optometrist for the total cost before making your final decision.

Facts About Frames

Spectacles are either made from metal, plastic, or carbon fibre. Most metal frames are made of coated nickel. New stronger plastics mean that frames can now be made thinner. If you are allergic to plastic, try hypoallergenic frames which are neutral in relation to the skin and unaffected by cosmetics. You can buy frames in every shape and size imaginable, from designer frames to budget conscious frames. If you can't find any frames to suit you, if you are a sportswoman, for example, you can probably have a pair of one off frames made especially for you. Your frames need to be comfortable. They should fit snugly over the bridge of your nose so that the weight of the spectacles is distributed evenly. If you have metal frames you can have special plastic comfort pads fitted.

Shape Up

Choosing glasses that suit you is terribly important. If you're not sure, don't rush a decision. Go away and think about it and if you can, take a friend back with you so you can get a second opinion. It helps if you

Round face shape

Heart face shape

Square face shape

Oval face shape

Oblong face shape

can look at yourself in a full length mirror so that you can take in your overall appearance. Take into consideration your face shape, hairstyle, colouring and lifestyle.

A round shaped face is characterised by full cheeks and chin with a rounded forehead. To reduce the roundness, go for straight lined frames such as square or rectangular shapes.

A heart shaped face is characterised by a wider forehead and cheekbones, tapering to a narrow pointed chin. Go for small delicate frames with the lower section fanning outwards away from the face.

A square shaped face is characterised by a wide forehead, a fairly straight line from the cheekbones to jaw and a square shaped chin. Balance this face shape by wearing soft round or oval frames.

An oval shaped face is considered the most ideal as it is perfectly proportioned. You'll find that most shaped frames will suit you, with smaller delicate designs looking best.

Oblong shaped faces tend to be narrow and long with a small forehead. Balance and reduce the length of the face by wearing wide frames with an upward curve.

Looking After Your Glasses

Never lay your glasses with the lenses down, you can scratch them. Keep your glasses in a good case so that they are protected at all times. Rinse your glasses in warm soapy water and dry with a soft cloth regularly. Get a special glasses cleaner for getting rid of smudges. Always make sure you have clean hands when handling your glasses.

Making-Up

Many people make the mistake of not bothering with eye make-up when they wear glasses. They think that because they're wearing glasses that their eyes can't be seen. Well, make-up is probably more important for spectacle wearers than for anyone else. Short-sighted people wear glasses that will make their eyes look smaller, so they need some careful shading to open up their eyes. Long-sighted people will have lenses that magnify the eyes. Care has to be taken when applying make-up, making sure that shades are blended really well, so that no harsh lines are showing.

If your eyes look small, sticking to one basic eye colour is best. Brushing it on in several different shades is the secret. Apply a pale colour to the lid and extend the colour to the brow area. Then apply a darker tone just above the natural socket line, intensifying at the outer corner. Brush a pale tone under the lower lashes. Finish the look with a smudge proof mascara. (Glasses wearers tend to rub their eyes a lot.)

If your eyes look big, apply your make-up with great care as your eyes are magnified. Any mistakes will be exaggerated because of this. Go for matt colours that will enhance the colour of your eyes and frames, because pearlised colours can look theatrical and too over the top. Brush a light coloured base across the lid, and fill in the socket line and below the lower lashes. Only use eyeliner pencils or liquids if you have a very steady hand. Dust your lashes and lids with loose powder. This will stop your make-up from creasing and will give it more staying power.

When wearing glasses, always inspect your eye make-up with your glasses on for the finished look, and tidy up any mistakes with cotton buds. You can eliminate that glassy look from your eyes and let your eyes be seen more clearly by having an anti-reflection coating on your lenses. It costs approximately fifteen pounds and is available from most opticians.

If you have sensitive eyes you should wear specially formulated cosmetics. Try Optique, Eye Care or Almay. When removing your eye make-up you should also choose brands for cleansing sensitive eyes. Try Klorane Eye Make-Up Remover Pads, Almay Non-Oily Eye Make-Up Remover or RoC Eye Make-Up Remover Gel.

Contact Lenses

If glasses really aren't for you, then maybe contact lenses are the answer. There are many types of contact lenses to choose from, but they all work basically in the same way. A contact lens is a paper thin shell like disc that fits over the coloured part of your eye. It floats on a film of tears and is held in place by surface tension.

The Eye Test

You are given a detailed test and examination of your eyes, eyelids, cornea and tear fluid. Then your tolerance level and suitability as a contact lens wearer can be assessed. Facts like whether you suffer from hay fever, how your eyes react to sunlight, cosmetics and cigarette smoke will also be taken into account. If you are prescribed lenses, you will be shown how to insert and remove them and you'll be given advice on their care.

Types of Lenses

Hard lenses are made of rigid plastic. They are tougher and longer lasting than soft lenses. Despite having the smallest surface area, for many users they can give the best vision. However, they have a long wearing in period, so you have to persevere through slight discomfort, and if the lenses aren't worn everyday it may mean going back to square one. Some people with very sensitive eyes are unable to wear hard lenses.

Gas-Permeable Hard Lenses are made from the same rigid plastic as hard lenses, but they allow oxygen to pass through them, allowing the eye to breathe. They are more comfortable than the usual hard lenses but they are easily scratched or torn. There's a thinner super gas-permeable lens which can be worn overnight.

Soft Lenses are the most comfortable. They are able to absorb water making them soft and flexible. Sixty per cent of contact lens wearers go for soft lenses. There are two types of soft lenses. The first consists of between thirty-eight and forty-two per cent water. The second has a higher content with seventy to eighty-five per cent water. Both require special care and must never be allowed to dry out.

Extended Wear Soft Lenses have a high water content. The recommended wearing time is up to a week, but their use must be carefully monitored by your optician for proper safety. They are useful for people who have difficulty in handling lenses on a daily basis.

Coloured Contact Lenses are a big fashion item. They're available in hard or soft form, and can be fitted without a prescription for the normal sighted. Soft lenses are best because they're the most comfortable. You can wear a different coloured pair each day to go with different coloured outfits. Opaque coloured contact lenses can literally turn brown eyes blue. All leading contact lens manufacturers make them, and they come in colours like violet, amber and even scarlet. To see what colour suits you best without having lenses fitted, try out a revolutionary computer used by some opticians. It freeze frames an image of your face so the coloured lenses of your choice can be painted into the eye area afterwards. Coloured contact lenses can also be used medicinally to cover up disfigured or scarred corneas. Transparent tinted lenses can change and brighten your existing eye colour, changing wishy washy blue to brilliant blue, or hazel to green.

Sports Lenses cover the whole of the visible eye area making them less likely to fall out. They're very suitable for swimmers.

Sunfiltered Lenses are a fairly new development made by Essilor. Soft lenses called Lunelle Solaire cut out glare and protect the eyes from ultraviolet light. They're useful for replacing sunglasses, and people involved in working outdoors or in sporting activities associated with water, sun or snow will find them particularly useful.

Making Up

If you're a contact lens wearer, always apply make-up after you've inserted your lenses, and remove your lenses before taking make-up off. Make sure that there's no grease, dirt or perfume on your fingers before touching your lenses. Get yourself a magnifying mirror. This will help with lens insertion and removal and will help you apply your make-up more accurately. The right texture of make-up is more important than colour when you're a contact lens wearer. Greasy eye creams, kohl pencils and crayons can end up sliding across your lenses and blurring your vision. Loose powders can be very painful. If any powder gets into your eyes it will irritate you like mad. Try powder pencils, applying them as solid colours for definition, then use a lighter shade to blend into them. Alternatively, go for a brand that is specifically designed for contact lens wearers.

Quick Tips

* If you're buying just one pair of glasses, avoid a bright colour or an outrageous shape. You'll find that you can only wear loud glasses with certain outfits, so go for something a bit more neutral instead.

* Glasses with a low set bridge will help shorten a long face.

* Glasses with a high set bridge will lengthen a short nose or shallow face.

* Make sure that your frames aren't so deep that they rest on your cheeks. They will be very uncomfortable to wear.

* If you have plump cheeks always go for shallow frames.

* To balance your eyes, the rim of your glasses should accommodate your eyebrows.

* If you have close-set eyes make them appear wider by wearing glasses with a clear bridge, graduating to a deeper colour at the outer edges.

* Make a short face look longer by having colour at the browline of the glasses, graduating to a clear lower rim.

* Make a round face look slimmer by having a concentrated colour on the bridge of your glasses, fading to the temples.

* If you can afford two pairs of glasses, have a practical pair for daytime and a more flamboyant pair for going out.

* If you like a pair of glasses that go against all the rules, buy them. Remember that rules are meant to be broken.

* If you're wearing lenses that magnify your eyes, apply your mascara subtly. You don't want it to look clogged.

* Cover up any bags that might be magnified with a concealer.

* Go for eye colours that complement the shade of your glasses and never bring your eye make-up out further than your frames.

Chapter Nine

Style File

People That Ooze Style

Annie Lennox
Paula Yates
Madonna
Elvis
James Dean
Paul Weller
Sean Connery
Paul Newman
Lauren Bacall
Katharine Hepburn
Yasmin Le Bon
Marilyn Monroe
Sade
Bryan Ferry
Marie Helvin
Beatrice Dalle
Mickey Rourke
Humphrey Bogart
Tom Cruise
Michael Jackson (when dancing)
Gordon T. Gopher
Superman
Jessica Rabbit
Dame Edna
Mickey Mouse

People With No Style

Jonathan Ross
Mandy Smith
Kylie Minogue
Jason Donovon
Bananarama
Gary Davies
Timmy Mallett
Phillip Schofield
Sam Fox
Cliff Richard
Shakin' Stevens
Boy George
Leigh Bowery
Tina Turner
Jim Bowen
Bob Monkhouse

Stylish Films

Breathless
Betty Blue
Gone With The Wind
Casablanca
West Side Story
Grease
Some Like It Hot
The Graduate
The Sting
Butch Cassidy and The Sundance Kid
Love Story

Stylish Cars

Karmann Ghia
Any convertible
Mercedes Sports
The Batmobile
Volkswagen Golf
Volkswagen Beetle
The car in Grease
Mk 2 Jag
BMW

Stylish Places

Paris
London
New York
Milan

Chapter Ten

Special Occasion Dressing

Dressing for a special occasion can be just as exciting as the event itself, but it can also cause us problems. To make the occasion as enjoyable as possible it is important to do a little research. Find out exactly what is in store at the event and then you can choose your clothes accordingly. Special occasions obviously need more thought and preparation than usual, so be organised. Give yourself plenty of time to pack or get ready for the special event. Don't leave anything until the last minute because a last minute panic will be the last thing you need.

Wedding Bells

When invited to a wedding one of the first thoughts that most girls think is what am I going to wear? It's the perfect excuse for treating yourself to something new and classy – after all weddings are very special occasions. If only it was really that simple though, life would be wonderful. We all know how difficult it can be to find an outfit that is just right for the occasion. You leave home in a good mood and five shops later you start to feel just a little bit fed up. The longer this goes on the more confused you will become, not knowing if it's the right style or colour for you.

The best thing to do is to decide on the colours that you really like to wear. The ones that suit you most. That will instantly save you time and energy because you can immediately disregard anything that isn't the right shade. Then decide on what shapes are the most flattering to you. Don't make the mistake of choosing something because it looks fussy and glamorous. It is so easy to get carried away and go over the top for a wedding. Good simple cuts always look best, especially in nice rich fabrics.

Choose something that you know you will wear again. A smart suit is always a good idea, because even if you don't wear suits very often you can wear the skirt with different shirts and tops. The same goes for the jacket. Smart jackets can look very stylish when worn with faded jeans for example. Keep jewellery to a minimum. Weddings aren't the place for bold jewellery. You don't want to attract attention to yourself with jingly bracelets in church.

Don't let the British weather ruin how you wear your outfit. Be prepared for it to be more chilly than it is warm. Instead of ruining an otherwise smart outfit with a cardigan or coat that doesn't match, go for layers of cosy underwear instead. Wear cute little vests and camisoles. Keep your make-up natural and make sure that your mascara is a good waterproof one, in case you shed the odd tear. Make sure that you blot your lipstick well too because weddings normally mean lots of kissing.

Gloves are a great accessory to wear at weddings. They can look very elegant. Tone them with your outfit for a nice sophisticated look. Finally, wear a hat, because it will add the finishing touch to your outfit. Even if you are unused to wearing one, make an effort and team it with your outfit. Remember that taller girls can wear much wider brimmed hats than small girls, so choose your hat accordingly and have a good wedding!

Party! Party!

Everybody loves a party – it's an occasion for dressing up to the nines. You can wear what you like to a party, whether it's a glamorous or sophisticated look. It all depends on the mood you're in. Take your time getting ready, decide on what you're going to wear and set your clothes out. Then choose your favourite make-up to go with your outfit. Lay your make-up out on a tray, and then have a hot luxurious bath, making sure that it is full of scented bubbles of course.

Go for rich fabrics like silk or velvet in deep or bright colours depending on your skin tone. Or wear your faithful little black dress that never lets you down. Lycra is a great fabric for parties that is very clingy and sexy *but only on the right figure please!* In fact any soft fabric clings, revealing your figure, so unless you want it revealed, go for more substantial fabrics.

If possible wear your hair in a different style, for impact. If it's long, try piling it all on top, or use bendy rollers and mousse, giving your hair lots of volume and bounce. If it's shorter try tonging it, or use straightening irons for a really sleek look. Wear your make-up a little heavier than usual because artificial lighting tends to drain the colour from your face. Go for more intense colours, stronger lipsticks and eye shadows with a bit of shimmer. Try a coloured mascara such as purple or bright blue.

Wear big bold jewellery. The bolder the better. Chunky gold or silver earrings or necklaces look good, but flamboyant costume jewellery looks best. Costume jewellery can be expensive but diamanté and crystals are great for catching the light making you look stunning. Wearing costume jewellery is also a great way of dressing up an otherwise dull dress or shirt.

Wear your tights dark and sheer for parties. Choose your shoes to go with your outfit. Shoes with a heel usually go best with party dresses, but flat shoes can look equally as sexy if you feel good in them. Bear in mind that if you're going to have a bit of a boogy, your feet will be happier in shoes that are soft and comfortable. Have fun!

In The Country

It's winter and you're going to the countryside with your boyfriend for a weekend. You're going to have to put a little bit of thought into what to take clotheswise. Just to confuse things more, you're going there to meet his parents. Eek! Well first of all try not to panic. Find out what's on the agenda and choose your clothes accordingly. Remember that what looks casual here can look very out of place in the country. Go for real country classics so you look the part.

Wear cords or your jeans for comfort (not the ones with the big rips in because I don't think his mum will be amused) and team them with a nice big Aran jumper. Get your jumper big and sloppy enough so that you can wear layers underneath to keep warm and make sure you take a good waterproof jacket. If you instantly think of an anorak or one of those sloane type jackets, think again. Waterproof jackets or coats no longer have to be naff. There are some very smart ones around. You can buy a mac in full length, three quarter length or a new short length, which looks really stylish. You should wear wellies but if you really can't bear to, go for a good waterproof pair of riding boots instead. Take a scarf, some gloves and a hat to keep warm.

Country folk do tend to dress practically during the day, so when there's an excuse for dressing up they don't let it pass them by. Don't make the mistake of packing just country casuals. Pack one classic dress, or a shirt and a pair of smart trousers in warm earthy colours. Take a cardigan too, in case the evenings are a bit chilly. Wear nice thick warm woolly socks with trousers or opaque tights instead of sheer ones to keep your legs warm. Go for nice chunky brogues in tan or rust, they're practical and smart. Finally, don't forget your thermals and your fleecy pyjamas.

Working Weekend

If you travel away for weekends with your work you will probably find the packing a real chore. After all, it's not as if you're packing for a fun holiday. Packing for a holiday can be fun, but for work you can't just throw anything you like into a case. You have to think of the events that will be taking place, and make sure that you have the right clothes to wear for the right events. This takes careful thought and planning. Wearing the right clothes to work is important in as much as they give you confidence. When meeting people for the first time, if you feel confident with the way you look you will probably handle things so much better. So what do you take on your weekend when you have to look efficient as well as immaculate?

Friday Evening

The important thing is to travel light. You won't look very professional if you turn up looking as if you've got everything but the kitchen sink with you. Try to match your briefcase or bag to your suitcase, giving yourself a smart co-ordinated appearance. Use a good quality case with a frame rather than a holdall for weekends. You will find that a case protects your clothes more, stopping them from creasing. You will also be shown more respect in hotels if you have smart baggage rather than a tatty looking bag.

Travel to your hotel in a smart suit but don't wear the jacket while travelling. Wear a smart jumper instead, because the jacket will crease if you sit around in it for long periods at a time. When you change for dinner, wear the suit with the jacket but a different top. Wear a top that is a bit dressier, and add earrings, a necklace and a brooch, dressing the outfit up even more. Keep your shoes the same all weekend.

For night-time don't forget your nightdress or pyjamas. If you take a dressing gown, take one in a silky fabric or a lightweight cotton. Other fabrics are bulkier and will take up too much room in your suitcase.

Saturday

Wear a lightweight knitted wool suit. Wool is great for packing because it doesn't crease, and lightweight wool doesn't take up too much room either. In the evening wear a dress in a lightweight crease-free fabric with the same jewellery as before.

Sunday

Travel home wearing the dress you wore on Saturday evening teamed with the jacket from your suit, giving it a more formal look.

Quick Tips

* Always allow yourself lots of time to get ready or to pack for a special occasion. Make sure that everything you need is clean, polished, or ironed, and that no buttons need sewing on. Do this a week before the event, not the night before.

* If you travel a lot, invest in a good case. It's worth buying one good case rather than buying lots of cheap ones.

* Buy yourself some little containers and bottles. You can fill them with your favourite toiletries like shampoo and moisturiser. Then when you travel away, you will not only save yourself time, but space in your suitcase.

* If an important outfit gets creased, hang it up in the bathroom while you take a shower. The steam will help the creases drop out.

* If you're a forgetful person, when travelling away, always make a list of what you need to take. That way you shouldn't forget anything important.

* Always pack extra tights in case you ladder a pair.

* Take a small drawstring bag for your dirty laundry.

* Never pack anything linen unless you take a good iron (a travel iron won't do) or have checked to see if the hotel has a pressing service.

* Try to carry your toiletries in a separate bag to your suitcase just in case there are any spillages.

* If you pack extra shoes, use shoe trees to help them keep their shape.

* Always pack shoes in a shoe bag or plastic bag. You don't want polish coming off and marking your clothes.

* Pack tailored clothes at the bottom of your suitcase.

* When folding a jacket, do the buttons up first so it keeps its shape. Fold it in two across the body, bringing the arms across the chest. If there are any obvious places that will crease, use tissue or polythene for padding out.

* Some items like T-shirts are less likely to crease if rolled rather than folded. Take a hair dryer or a travel hairdryer. Not all hotels have them.

Chapter Eleven

The Style Guide Quiz

What's Your Style?

Find out if you ooze style by doing this fun quiz.

1. You go shopping to buy an outfit for a friend's wedding. What do you choose from the choice below?

A) A Prince of Wales check jacket and matching skirt.
B) Anything as long as it has a designer label.
C) A white suit.
D) A pair of shoes, a hat and a jacket that you can wear with several items that you already have in your wardrobe.

2. While you're out, you buy a wedding present too. Do you choose –

A) Microwave cookware, assuming that they have a microwave.
B) A cappuccino maker.
C) A doorbell that plays ten different tunes.
D) An original hand-painted frame for the couple to put one of their wedding photos in.

3. What colours do you like wearing most?

A) Subtle colours like grey or white, for example.
B) Just black.
C) Orange, lime, pale pink, in fact all colours.
D) Bright primaries.

4. What is your favourite accessory?

A) Two items: a Filofax and a Rolex.
B) A pair of Raybans.
C) A Garfield badge.
D) A collection of silver rings.

5. What is your favourite item of clothing?

A) A raincoat.
B) Your latest buy, which was yesterday.
C) You haven't really got one.
D) A skirt that you made yourself.

6. What is organza?

A) An unpractical and see-through fabric?
B) This season's fabric?
C) An illness?
D) A very versatile fabric that can be used in a variety of ways?

7. How much money do you spend on clothes each month?

A) You don't buy clothes every month. You buy good quality expensive suits which last a long time.
B) Most of your monthly salary, and sometimes all of it on just one item.
C) Not a lot. You buy most of your clothes in the sales.
D) Hardly anything. You make most of your clothes or customise second-hand stuff from jumble sales.

8. What do you look for when buying an outfit?

A) Something smart and practical.
B) Something very current. Preferably with the label on the outside.
C) A bargain.
D) Something that is well made and well cut.

9. What do you want for Christmas?

A) A satellite dish.
B) Money, so that you can spend it on clothes.
C) A ring with your initials on it.
D) A new sewing machine.

10. What are shoe trees?

A) An object that goes into your shoes and helps them keep their shape when you're not wearing them?
B) A waste of time because your shoes are too expensive not to wear.
C) Evergreen trees with shoe shaped leaves.
D) Not necessary as far as you're concerned, you always use socks which do exactly the same job.

Mostly As

If you scored mostly As then you are definitely a 'yuppie'. You are very work orientated and love status symbols like your Filofax and very flash watches. A flash watch is probably more important to you than any of your other jewellery because it has a name on it which spells success. You see, any other type of jewellery could be bought for you as a present, whereas your watch is more likely to have been bought by you. You're intent on making your fortune so that you can surround yourself with life's riches. Make sure that you're around to enjoy them and remember, all work and no play makes a 'yuppie' a dull girl.

Mostly Bs

If you scored mostly Bs then you're what's called a 'fashion victim'. You're well-known for saying things like 'is that this season's or last season's Gaultier?'. You know what you're going to spend your month's salary on even before you've been paid, and you're forever in debt because there's always something else you have to buy. Slow down a bit, and consider whether you're buying the clothes because they look good on you, or just because you're impressed by the label.

Mostly Cs

If you scored mostly Cs then I'm afraid you haven't even got a name. The only thing you could be called is a 'mess', you've simply got no style at all. For starters, you should never wear white to somebody else's wedding, and haven't you ever wondered why some of your clothes make you look ill? That's because you're paying no attention to your skin colouring and what colours suit you. You can't just wear a colour because you like it, you know. You need to take fashion a bit more seriously if you want to get some style. I hope that you did this quiz before reading the book. If not, I suggest you read the book again. Oh and lastly, I gather that you're a fan of Garfield. If you have one of those Garfields with the suckers on its paws in your car window, take it off now!

Mostly Ds

If you scored mostly Ds then you're an 'individualist'. Some people are born with style, while others simply acquire it as they get older. Whatever the case, you have it. In fact you set your own style and people look to you in admiration. You don't necessarily follow fashion, but choose clothes that you look and feel good in instead. Your secret is not trying too hard. You take fashion seriously, but not too seriously. Think yourself lucky, because you're the envy of lots of people. You have the knack of putting literally anything together and making it look good.

Chapter Twelve

Dos and Don'ts

Useful Style Tips

Do:

Remember that accessories can dress your look up or down.

Wear vertical stripes if you are short, they will make you look taller.

Buy a top to go with that skirt you've just bought. It's better to have the skirt with you to ensure a perfect match.

Choose bold jewellery and wide brimmed hats if you are tall.

Wear V necks, horse shoe, or scoop necks if your neck is short.

Make sure that your top isn't too tight, and that you wear a good fitting bra if you are big busted.

Wear a padded bra to make a small bust look bigger.

Stick with loose fitting sleeves if you have chunky arms.

Wear clothes with a wide waistband if you have a long waist.

Wear long lined jackets and jumpers if you have a big bottom and big hips.

Choose shoes with a bit of a heel if you have short legs.

Make sure that your clothes don't swamp you if you're small.

Go for bold prints and stripes if you are tall.

Make sure that your trousers are a good length if your legs are long.

Avoid wearing long earrings if you have a short neck.

Wear jackets and tops with square shoulders if your own shoulders are narrow.

Pin your bra straps to the inside of slash neck tops to stop them showing.

Draw attention away from bad areas. For example wear nice trousers to draw the eye away from a big bust.

Wear an attractive bracelet to draw the eye away from chubby upper arms.

Stick with skirts and trousers with a narrow waistband if your waist is short.

Wear cropped jackets if your waist is long.

Wear loose fitting clothes if your waist is big.

Try wearing little skating skirts over cycling shorts or leggings to hide big bottoms.

Wear jewellery and interesting tops if you have big hips, to draw the attention away from them.

Avoid trousers if you have a big bottom.

Wear roomy trousers if you have big legs.

Try a highly cut swimsuit to make short legs look longer.

Keep your clothes unfussy if you are on the short side.

Wear short skirts if you are short, to make your legs look longer.

Avoid anything with a large print and too much detail, like big pockets and zips, if you are small.

Wear dramatic flared coats if you are tall.

Go for clothes in the same colour but different shades to create the illusion of height.

Select belts in toning colours rather than contrasting. If you are short, contrasting colours break up the body line making you appear shorter.

Wear clothes with ruffles and flounces and lots of detail if you are tall and slim.

Keep shirts unbuttoned at the top if you have a short neck.

Wear wide round collars and ruffles on the shoulders if your shoulders are sloping.

Stick with neat vertical jackets if you want to hide a big bust.

Wear three quarter length jackets if you are chubby.

Choose tops with fullness if you have a small chest.

Try unbelted styles or drop waisted dresses if your waist is thick or short.

Go for chunky jumpers and cardigans if you have a small bust.

Wear wrapover skirts if you have big hips.

Keep dresses or skirts to the midcalf if you have big legs.

Select narrow trousers with cropped jackets if you have short legs.

Wear wide lapels if you have a small bust.

Pick shoes with a medium or low heel if you have big legs. Big legs look too heavy in high heels.

Wear fitted styles if you have a good figure. Why not show it off?

Disguise a small bust by wearing horizontal stripes to give you more curves.

Match your tights to your shoes to make your legs look slimmer.

Wear hats – but only with confidence! Otherwise you won't be able to carry it off.

Try layers of clothing like shirts, waistcoats and jackets to cover a small bust.

Don't:

Wear bulky layers if you are small.

Pick anything that is too girly if you are tall.

Choose polo necks, mandarin collars or anything high necked if your neck is short.

Buy a top just because it looks good on a friend. It may not suit you.

Wear long coats if you are small. Choose three quarter lengths instead.

Leave it until the last minute to buy something for a special occasion. You'll probably buy something completely out of character.

Wear wide legged trousers if you are short.

Dress in off the shoulder or sleeveless tops if you have a big bust.

Wear bulky fabrics if you have big hips.

Select small jewellery or accessories if you are tall.

Wear short necklaces if you have a short neck.

Try wearing wide or tight belts if you have a big bust.

Wear anything with bold prints if you are small.

Contemplate wearing neck scarves if you have a short neck.

Wear long jumpers or jackets if you have short legs.

Consider stone or marble wash jeans which are naff. Let your jeans fade naturally instead.

Carry a large shoulder bag if you are small.

Wear suits with short skirts and jackets if you are tall.

Have your haircut in a short severe style if your neck is short.

Wear wide trousers or skirts if you have narrow shoulders, otherwise you'll look pear shaped.

Tower in high heels if you are tall. Go for medium heels instead.

Wear fitted tops if you have narrow shoulders.

Select dark underwear under white or pastel colours. It looks awful and tarty. Wear white, pastel or skintone underwear instead.

Wear drop waisted dresses if you have short legs.

Choose ribbed jumpers if you have sloping shoulders.

Wear sheer or organza tops if you have a big bust.

Stoop if you are tall. Be proud of your height and walk tall.

Hunch your shoulders if you have a big bust. You will only draw attention to yourself.

Wear figure hugging clothes if you have a small bust.

Try fitted sleeves if you have big arms.

Wear high waisted skirts or trousers if you have a small waist.

Go for drop waisted dresses if you have a long waist.

Wear sleeveless tops if you have big arms.

Choose ballet cardigans if you have a big bust.

Wear belted clothes if you have a big waist.

Swamp yourself with wide belts if you have a short waist. You'll look like you've got no waist at all.

Wear narrow trousers like ski pants or pedal pushers if you have a big bottom.

Try thick woolly tights if you have big legs.

Wear vertical striped tops if you are long waisted.

Wear fitted jumpers or blouses if you have a big waist.

Select anything that clings if you have a big bottom.

Wear clothes that are gathered at the waist if your waist is big.

Try wearing your trousers tucked into your boots if you have short legs.

Wear clothes that are too small or too big for you.

Consider a mini skirt if your legs are big.

Pick short or midcalf boots if you have short or big legs.

Wear wide belts if you have a big waist.

Select black tights to wear with white shoes. It looks dreadful.

Wear cropped jumpers or jackets if you have a big bottom.

Drape yourself with too much gold jewellery. It looks really tacky.

Wear shorts if your bottom is big.

Chapter Thirteen

Clothes Care

If you care about your appearance, it's important that you look after your clothes. By spending a couple of minutes each day, you can organise your wardrobe so that your life runs more smoothly. It's very easy to get ready for bed and to leave your clothes where you've taken them off, instead of hanging them up. Especially if it's been a long day and you're tired. But what happens when you next want to wear that outfit? You spend ages pressing it when really it could have been avoided, if only you'd hung it up.

So is it worth it? Simple clothes care doesn't take up that much of your time. Just a couple of minutes each day will keep you looking immaculate, and you'll probably find that you save yourself money too. It's the same with most things, by looking after your clothes and treating them well they will last longer.

Storing Your Clothes

Most people find that no matter how much space they have for storing clothes it's never enough. If you're one of these people then you have to get organised. It's important that your clothes are clearly visible. Otherwise, you will forget about the existence of some items, not getting as much wear out of them as possible.

If you're really short of space it's a good idea to sort your clothes into two categories. During the winter, pack away all your summer clothes, and do the same in the summer. Make sure that your clothes are well protected and won't collect dust. Wrap them in tissue (white, because coloured tissue can stain if it gets wet) or polythene, and store them in a suitcase or a trunk if you have one. When you do this it's a good chance to have a sort out at the same time. Don't hang on to clothes that you haven't worn for ages. Be honest and ask yourself if you're ever likely to wear them again. If the answer is no, give them away to a friend, relative or charity. You'll be making someone else happy and giving yourself more storage space.

Once you've packed away your summer clothes, review your storage situation. Maybe you need more space, because your winter wardrobe has increased from last year. If you can't afford another wardrobe, maybe there's a spare cupboard that you could get a rail fitted into. If not, buy yourself a clothes rail which you can pick up really cheaply. The only disadvantage with a clothes rail is that your clothes can get rather dusty. The best thing to do to solve this problem is to cover your clothes in long polythene bags. Keep the ones that come with your dry cleaning. (Never keep fur, suede or leather stored in polythene bags. Skins sweat when enclosed in plastic and can go mouldy, so use a fabric bag instead.) If you haven't got many long polythene bags use the rail for hanging your most frequently worn clothes so they are washed regularly, and not allowed to collect dust.

If your clothes are squashed into a wardrobe they will look a mess, being full of creases. When too many clothes are squashed together like this they don't have room to breathe so allow lots of space between your clothes for the air to circulate. If you need more storage space for jumpers, you could buy yourself some wide shelving. Try covering shelves with a blind to keep the dust out. When you hang clothes in your wardrobe have a system. Keep the clothes that you don't wear very often at the back of your wardrobe, making sure that they are covered up. Then hang all your dresses together, then your trousers, and so on. Keep all the same colours together, it makes it quicker when choosing your clothes.

If you have the room, hang your shirts up rather than folding them. Never hang up anything knitted, it will sag and stretch, losing its shape. Always use good clothes hangers never wire ones. Wooden, plastic or fabric ones are best. When hanging something up, make sure that you do up the zip or buttons so that the garment keeps its shape. Check that the shoulders are evenly placed on the hanger and that the garment is hanging correctly. Make sure the hanger is not pushing out the shoulders or sleeves as this will cause a bump. Use padded hangers on delicate fabrics. Use clamp hangers for pleated skirts, they will help make the skirt hang straight. Make sure that the creases in trousers are correctly aligned to avoid double creases. Wooden hangers with a serrated bar covered in rubber are ideal for trousers because they will not slip off. Before hanging anything up, empty out the pockets, things left in pockets can make a garment lose its shape.

Never cram too many clothes in your drawers, otherwise they will crease. Line drawers just in case there are any wood splinters which can damage clothes, and keep sachets of lavender in your underwear drawer for sweet smelling undies. Store your accessories where they are easily seen. Keep scarves in a neat pile so you can match them to different outfits. Hang your belts from the buckle. Never roll or fold them because they can crack. Keep your jewellery on show. Or use a different box for earrings and one for necklaces and so on. You can also store jewellery in pretty baskets or tins. Keep hats in their boxes to prevent them from getting dusty. Stuff the crowns with paper so that they keep their shape. If you have any bags that you're not using, make sure that you stuff them too. Store your shoes in a shoe rack or at the bottom of your wardrobe. Never stack them on top of one another, and never put them away if they're muddy or damp.

Washing and Dry Cleaning

Before washing or cleaning a garment, always check the label for washing and care instructions. The washing symbols are sometimes a bit difficult to understand – you can always check them on the charts that are on the back of soap powder packets. Don't be tempted to wash anything that says 'Dry Clean Only', because if you ruin it, it will be entirely your fault. If you hand or machine wash something, always make sure you use the right water temperature. Sort your washing into the water temperature required and into colours. Always wash highly coloured garments separately.

Treat wool with care and only machine wash it if the label says so. Dry woollens flat and never tumble dry. Don't wring them either. Get rid of any excess water by rolling the garment in a towel and squeezing. Some clothes get creased up when they are spun dry, so you could use this method on them. Never tumble dry a garment if it has lost its label, it could shrink.

Good dry cleaning will preserve an outfit's shape, prolonging its life and keeping it fresh. If there's a particular mark or stain on an outfit it is worth pointing it out to the dry cleaner. Always use a specialist cleaner for suede or leather garments. But don't wait until a garment gets stained before taking it to the cleaners. If it's dark it probably doesn't look very dirty but cleaning is necessary for removing grime that gets caught in the fibres.

Ironing and Pressing

To achieve good results you have to iron on a proper ironing board. Sleeve boards are very useful too. Being in a hurry and ironing on a work surface won't do. It's a good idea when ironing, to have at hand a water spray for dampening fabrics and a large cotton hanky for pressing. Make sure the hanky is white in case the colour runs. Use ozone-friendly spray starch. It is very good for cotton and linen.

Always follow the label instructions and move the iron temperature gauge accordingly. Iron delicate fabrics under a hanky and iron on the inside of garments that might go shiny. Always iron seams and hems on the inside. Never put anything on immediately after it's been ironed. If the fabric is still warm it will crease instantly, undoing all of your hard work. Smooth out bows and ribbon trimmings on your underwear while it's still damp. Then it will dry crease free.

Mishaps

If you have a mishap and spill something on your clothes you have to act very quickly. Don't ignore the stain because then you might never get it out. There are lots of efficient stain removers on the market. However, if a stain remover doesn't do the trick and the garment is washable, you should put it into luke warm water as soon as possible. Make sure the water isn't too hot or it could set the stain.

If the garment isn't washable there are lots of remedies you can try. If it's a greasy stain, soak it up with talcum powder. If it's a fruit or wine stain, try salt which will help absorb the colour. Other marks can be rubbed gently with a damp cloth, but don't wet the garment too much or you could end up with a water mark.

If all else fails, your only other alternative is the dry cleaners. Take the garment to the best dry cleaners you can afford and make sure you point out the stain, telling him what it is.

Repairs

If a garment needs repairing, don't hang it up and say that you'll tend to it later. The chances are you will forget, and before you know where you are, you have five or more items to repair. Always do any repairing straight away. That way everything that is in your wardrobe will be wearable and you won't have to put off wearing one of your favourite outfits, or do a rush repair job. It's a good idea to carry a mini repair kit in your bag. Just a needle and some thread in a variety of colours will do the trick. Safety pins are a good idea too, just in case you lose a button.

Brushing

After you've worn your clothes a few times give them a good brush. Most people rarely brush their clothes, but it's good to. Brushing removes dust and particles of dirt that can become embedded in the clothes fibres, and even tear them. A good brushing will make your clothes look nice and fresh. Lay your clothes flat and brush in semi-circular movements. Brush against the nap to clean the fabric, and then with the grain leaving a smooth finish. If you're in a hurry and want to get rid of fluff from an outfit, try Sellotape.

Shoe Care

Your feet can distort your shoes if worn every day. Give your shoes time to rest by alternating them. Use a barrier cream on your shoes to protect them against water. Polish your shoes regularly and it will prolong their life. If you can, polish your shoes in the evening. The polish can then feed your shoes overnight. Use proper shoe polish and a brush and clean your shoes in the traditional way for best results. Remove any caked on mud with a stiff brush. Brush suede and canvas shoes regularly to prevent dust and dirt working into the fabric. Use a soft brush or a rubber brush. A wire brush will destroy the surface of your shoes and could tear them.

When you take off your shoes, use shoe trees so that they keep their shape, or alternatively stuff socks into the foot of your shoes once they have cooled down. Make sure that you have your shoes heeled regularly, and always have rubber soles rather than leather, they last longer. If your shoe is hard to get on, don't force it. You could break its back. Ease your shoe on by using a shoe horn, or if you don't have one, a teaspoon will do.

Accessory Care

Accessories need just as much looking after as your clothes. Turn your bag out regularly. Most people tend to accumulate lots of rubbish in their bags, carrying around unnecessary weight. Using Sellotape, get rid of any fluff that has settled into the folds of the bag lining. Clean the outside of your bag, but if it is leather use polish sparingly. Buff it up with a soft cloth, removing any traces of colour that could rub off onto your clothes. Clean hats, gloves, scarves and belts regularly. They need looking after just like the rest of your clothing if they are going to set off an outfit.

Chapter Fourteen

Questions and Answers

As Fashion Editor of *Mizz* magazine, I get many letters asking for advice on fashion. Here I answer some of the most frequently asked questions and some of the more interesting ones.

Q. Can you please help me because I am very confused. I went shopping recently, and in some shops I was a size ten while in others I was a size twelve. How can this be?

A. Clothes sizes do vary, and a lot depends on how much you spend on them. Good clothes benefit from a more generous cut. If you pay a lot of money for a garment it will always have a more generous cut with ample hems and seams. There is a reason for this, so let me explain. If you imagine that all the garments in a shop were at one stage just a sample. (A sample is a garment made up from the original design specification.) It is from this sample that the garments which you see on the shop floor are developed. A sample is carefully costed which means that somebody works out exactly how much the garment will cost to produce. Taken into account is: the number of processes involved in the making, the man hours required and the amount of material used. The garment being made will have a budget which it must not go over. One of the easiest and most effective ways of keeping something within budget is to use the smallest amount of fabric that you can get away with. The shoulders, sleeves and bodice of a garment can all be narrowed a little, and the waist and skirt can also be reduced a little if need be. The hem and the overlaps at the seam might also be slightly reduced. So you see, if the garment is being made to fit a size ten for example, the reduced version will in fact be a size ten, it will just be very close fitting. As I said earlier, this process of cutting down on the fabric takes place at the cheaper end of the market where there is a strict budget. So if I were you, I would say that I was a size ten in well cut garments, and a size twelve in cheap and cheerful garments.

Q. I want to be a model. My friends at school say that I'm pretty, and I think I've got what it takes. The only thing is, I don't know how to go about getting into the modelling profession. I've heard that you have to be very tall, but I don't know the exact height. Can you give me some advice and tell me how to get started?

A. A fashion model's life usually starts at the age of fourteen to sixteen. However, some fashion models start younger, while others start older. You have to be a minimum of five foot eight inches tall. You will also need to have good even features, healthy skin and hair, and a good figure. You'll have to be photogenic and have good stamina and personality. Modelling isn't as glamorous as it seems. Sometimes it means standing for hours in the freezing cold, having to look warm and pretending you're having a brilliant time when you're not. It can be very hard work. Most people associate modelling with making lots of money. However, only a handful of models make their fortune. There is lots of competition in the modelling world, so it can be very hard to make it to the top. A fashion model's career is very short lived too. It normally ends from the mid to late twenties. There are exceptions to this of course, because you can go on to do older modelling, but work seems to slow down as you get older.

A model agency will need to see pictures of you before they take you on, because they need to see if you are photogenic. However, this doesn't mean paying lots of money for a portfolio of pictures. There are lots of so called professional photographers around that are ready to take your picture for an exorbitant fee. Don't fall into this trap. Snap shot pictures are all your agency will need at this stage. If a good agency thinks that you have potential, they will take you on, not charging you any money at this point. It's a bad sign if an agency takes you on and instantly asks for money for you to appear in their book or on their headsheet. What generally happens is this: Your agency will set up test shoots for you. A test shoot is where a photographer that is still working on his portfolio takes your picture. There is normally a hairdresser and a make-up artist as well, and all of you work together because you all want photographs for your portfolios. The only money you will have to pay out, will be to get prints made up from the transparencies or contact sheets. Your agency will send you on lots of appointments with photographers and set up as many test shoots for you as they can. They will also groom you and teach you how to take care of your looks. Then, once they feel that your portfolio is looking good, they'll send you on appointments to editorial offices hoping that you will get magazine work. This is where a model's career usually begins. Editorial work can be fun, but it is the lowest paid. However it does have its good points, there can be lots of travel to exotic countries involved.

If you are still interested in becoming a model, phone the Association of Model Agencies for a list of phone numbers and addresses. Remember that you shouldn't have to pay a joining fee when being taken on by an agency. The only expenses you should incur initially, are for an A–Z of London, a Travel Card because you'll have to do lots of travelling and any pictures that you want printed up.

Q. I spend quite a bit of money on my clothes. If I see a garment that is a bit pricey, if I like it, I don't mind paying for it. However, I do mind when after a couple of washes the garment needs repairing. The other day I was about to buy a shirt when two girls were looking at the same shirt. The first girl frowned and said to her friend that she'd never pay that price for something that was so badly made.

How could she tell that it was badly made? If I know then maybe I can shop more wisely in the future.

A. Good quality garments are usually made from a high percentage of natural fibre. To check a garment's quality, first turn the garment inside out – and don't let the funny looks from shop assistants put you off. Look to see if it has been made with a generous cut and check how the seams have been finished, making sure they are not ragged. If the seams have been clipped in tiny zig zags to prevent fraying, the garment will not have as long a life as one where the seams have been oversewn. Check that any pocket edges have been finished properly and that there are no loose threads. If there is a zip, make sure that it is the correct weight for the fabric and that it is well concealed, closing neatly at the top. Check that it runs smoothly up and down, and that it has not been inserted so close to the edge that the material catches in the teeth during use. It should lie flat and not pucker the smooth line of the seam. Look at the lining that should be soft and roomy. Top quality garments don't have the lining hanging free at the hem, it is properly inserted and joined at the base. Check that patterns match at the side seams. Stripes across the body should match the stripes on the sleeves. The yoke at the back should not interrupt the pattern, and the pattern should match on the pockets of shirts too. If there is any top stitching check that it is even and straight. If there are button holes, make sure that they have been finished off properly and check that buttons align with their corresponding holes.

If you want to check the fabric of a garment, you can see if it is of good quality by rubbing it with your fingers. A good quality fabric should show no sign of rubbing. You should also pull the seams sharply from either side. The threads will gape and stretch if the fabric is of poor quality. If you want to see if a fabric will crease, scrunch it up tightly for a few seconds. A good crease free fabric will recover quickly when released. To see if a fabric is too static, rub it between your fingers for a few seconds. If the fabric sticks to your fingers, the synthetic percentage is too high and the garment will cling. The cheaper a garment is, the more you have to examine it. Items like skirts that are made with too small an amount of fabric with small hems, will obviously not hang as well as a skirt with ample fabric. Having said this however, you can pay large amounts for some designer items and still not get perfectly made goods, so always examine a garment before buying it. Remember that cheap clothes are cheap because of the economic methods used. By skimping on the quality, up to the minute clothes are produced at a price that we can all afford. So, if you are buying something very cheap, don't forget that it is only meant to be cheap and cheerful and that better quality clothes for important occasions cost more.

Q. I have just left school and I have three white shirts that are in absolutely perfect condition. I was going to give them away, but then I thought if I wrote to you, maybe you would be able to give me some advice on how to jazz them up.

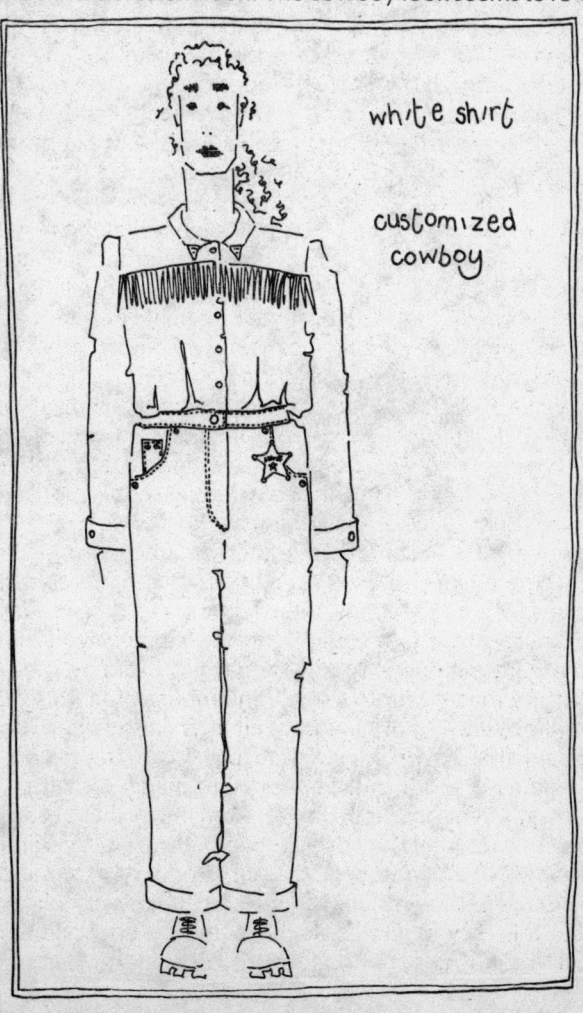

A. If I were you I would only customise two of the shirts. Everybody should have one good basic white shirt in their wardrobe. You will find a plain white shirt invaluable. It can be worn with so many different outfits for different looks. I always wear mine with my favourite red blazer and jeans for a classic but casual look. There are numerous ways of customising the other two. I think that I would give one of the shirts a western look. The cowboy look seems to re-emerge every season so that's quite a safe look. Get yourself some black fringing which is available from most haberdashery departments, and sew it on to the seam that runs across the back of the shirt near the top, and the seams that run across the shoulders. Add some collar tips and a sheriff's badge to complete the look.

The second shirt could be given a real fun look. You can dye it if you wish, using one of those dyes that go in the washing machine, or

white shirt

pattern power

you could keep it white. Draw with a pencil a pattern of your choice. It can be anything you like, mad squiggles, flowers or even star shapes. If you haven't got a very steady hand, maybe you could make up a stencil with some card and use this. Once you've finished your design, using a special fabric pen or pens in the colours of your choice, go over the pencil marks. It's best to use a stencil for big areas like stars, you can place the stencil over the shape and just fill in with

white shirt

casual but classic

the pen. These pens are available from most department stores. Make sure that you insert a card between the shirt layers or the colour could run through to the other side. Once the shirt is dry, you can wear it and wash it as many times as you wish, and the pattern will stay put.

Q. I'm going to a party at the end of the month. Everybody is going well over the top saying that they're wearing party frocks, the works. The problem is I'm really short of cash. Where can I get a really special party dress at a good price?

A. I think your best bet is to go for something second-hand. Look in your local second-hand shops, go to jumble sales and antique markets and something amazing will turn up. You can pick up some beautiful old dresses with lovely antique lace detail. Or you can go for something fifties and fun, worn with a huge petticoat underneath for fullness. When you look at second-hand garments you have to learn to look past the grubbiness. A good clean can work wonders.

You should also look at dresses that perhaps need livening up a little (maybe one that's already in your wardrobe). You don't need to be good at sewing to do this either. Simple alterations can change a boring dress into an amazing one. If a dress looks a little frumpy, see how different it could look by taking it up a couple of inches. If it has a belt it will probably be a cheap and nasty one. Imagine how it could look with one of your belts instead. Maybe the buttons need changing. Sometimes not enough thought goes into the buttons on an outfit and the outfit can be ruined. Try changing them. Anyone can sew a few buttons on, and it's incredible how an outfit can be completely transformed just by doing this.

If you're feeling really daring, why not choose a plain dress and sew on some sparkly sequins. They're available from most haberdashery departments and only need a couple of stitches. Whatever you decide, I bet that even wearing a second-hand dress, or an old dress, you'll be the best dressed there. Your outfit will be the most original, and there's another added bonus too. You won't have to worry about anyone at the party wearing the same dress as you.

Q. I don't have much money to spend on clothes, so when I do spend money, I want to spend it on something that won't be out of fashion two months later. At the same time I want to look stylish. What do you suggest?

A. By owning just a few garments you can have just as much style as anyone else. In fact, some people own too many clothes and when they get ready, they try too hard to look good. Everything is too thought out, not allowing their individuality to shine through. Style is individuality. Don't be so intent on buying the latest item that is in fashion, because it may not suit you. You shouldn't let current fashion swamp your personality. Learn what works for you and stick to it. Buy something fashionable by all means, but only if you feel good in it, and only if you think it won't date too quickly. There are sometimes items that go in and out of fashion very quickly, and these are usually obvious. Take the puffball skirt for one. If you're not sure, stick to classic garments instead and you can't go wrong.

Q. I bought a pair of shoes in the sale. They were marked as 'seconds' because they had a mark on the suede. I wore them once and where the mark was a tear appeared. I took them back to the shop but they wouldn't do a thing. As you can understand I was very annoyed and upset. Aren't they obliged to give me a new pair?

A. No. I'm afraid that you're lumbered with a pair of faulty shoes. The fact that they were marked as 'seconds' means that you have no redress with the manufacturer. In future when you buy something in the sale, don't get carried away. People tend to buy things just because they're cheap and they never wear them. You however are unfortunate, you bought a pair of shoes that no doubt you would have got wear from if they hadn't split. You've learnt your lesson the hard way. In future when you buy something that is a 'second', make sure that you inspect it more carefully. If you can't see a fault, get a shop assistant to tell you exactly what is wrong with the item. Then only buy the item if you can disguise, correct or live with the fault. If you'd looked a little closer at your shoes, maybe you would have seen that the mark was a weakness in the material. Then what was supposed to have been a bargain, might not have been an expensive mistake.

THE JUNK FOOD VEGETARIAN

JONATHAN CAINER

Whole food fanatics have had it their own way too long!

If you want to spend your life boiling beans, riding bicycles and getting 'back to the earth' you can join them.

But if your desire to be a vegetarian is NOT tied up with fear of technology, a love of washing up or a fetish for beansprouts – tuck in.

This book is dedicated to everyone who likes canned soup, frozen pizzas, processed peas, packet curries and instant whip. Remember –

Carry your can-opener with pride!

'The answer to all my dreams! At last a vegetarian cook book that isn't all millet and mung beans'
Jackie

'Entertaining and useful'
MS London

LIGHTNING

SAFE, STRONG AND STREETWISE

HELEN BENEDICT

SAFE, STRONG AND STREETWISE takes a bold look at some of the problems faced by teenagers today. What is sexual abuse? How can you defend yourself against it? Who can you turn to for help and advice? How should you react if you are physically attacked? All these important questions and more are answered in a realistic and constructive way, using accounts given by young people about difficult situations they have had to face.

'It's the ultimate street-safety guide.'

Lenny Henry

LIGHTNING

POST A LITTLE HAPPINESS

Post·A·Book

A Royal Mail service in association with the Book Marketing Council & The Booksellers Association.

Post·A·Book is a Post Office trademark.